AAT

ASSESSMENT KIT

Intermediate Unit 6

Cost Information

In this May 2002 edition

- Kit updated in the light of the assessor's review of the previous edition of this Kit
- New guidance on the preparation of portfolios
- The kit is up to date for developments in the subject as at 1 April 2002
- Practice activities
- Two Practice Devolved Assessments
- One Trial Run Devolved Assessment
- The AAT's Sample Simulation for this Unit
- Three Trial Run Central Assessments for this Unit
- The December 2001 Central Assessment to attempt as a 'mock' under exam conditions

FOR 2002 AND 2003 SKILLS BASED AND EXAM BASED ASSESSMENTS

BPP Publishing

May 2002

First edition 1999
Fourth edition May 2002

ISBN 0 7517 6425 6 (Previous edition 0 7517 6238 5)

British Library Cataloguing-in-Publication Data
A catalogue record for this book
is available from the British Library

Published by

BPP Publishing Limited
Aldine House, Aldine Place
London W12 8AW

www.bpp.com

Printed in Great Britain by W M Print
45-47 Frederick Street
Walsall, West Midlands
WS2 9NE

We are grateful to the Lead Body for Accounting for permission to reproduce extracts from the Standards of Competence for Accounting.

CONTENTS

Lecturers' resource pack activities are practice activities and assessments for lecturers to set in class or for homework. The answers are given in the BPP Lecturers' Resource Pack.

BPP
PUBLISHING

HOW TO USE THIS ASSESSMENT KIT

Aims of this Assessment Kit

To provide the knowledge and practice to help you succeed in assessments for Intermediate Unit 6 *Recording Cost Information.*

To succeed in the assessments you need a thorough understanding in all areas covered by the standards of competence.

To tie in with the other components of the BPP Effective Study Package to ensure you have the best possible chance of success.

Interactive Text This covers all you need to know for the assessments for Unit 6 *Recording Cost Information.* Icons clearly mark key areas of the text. Numerous activities throughout the text help you practise what you have just learnt.
Assessment Kit When you have understood and practised the material in the Interactive Text, you will have the knowledge and experience to tackle this Assessment Kit for Unit 6 *Recording Cost Information*. This Assessment Kit aims to get you through the central assessment and the devolved assessment, whether in the form of the AAT Simulation or in the workplace.
Passcards These short memorable notes are focused on key topics for Unit 6, designed to remind you of what the Interactive Text has taught you.

Recommended approach to this assessment kit

(a) To achieve competence in all units, you need to be able to do **everything** specified by the standards. Study the text very carefully and do not skip any of it.

(b) Learning is an **active** process. Do **all** the activities as you work through the text so you can be sure you really understand what you have read.

(c) After you have covered the material in the Interactive Text, work through this **Assessment Kit**.

(d) Try the **Practice Activities.** These are linked into each chapter of the Interactive Text, and are designed to reinforce your learning and consolidate the practice that you have had doing the activities in the Interactive Text. Depending on their difficulty, they are graded as Pre-assessment or Assessment.

(e) Then attempt the **Practice Devolved Assessments**. These are designed to test your competence in certain key areas of the Standards of Competence and will give you practice at completing a number of tasks based upon the same data.

(f) Next do the **Trial Run Devolved Assessment**. It is designed to cover the areas you might see when you do a full devolved assessment.

(g) Next try the AAT's **Sample Simulation** which gives you the clearest idea of what a full devolved assessment will be like.

(h) Then try the Trial Run Central Assessments. They will give you a good idea of what you will meet in the 'real thing'.

(i) **Try the December 2001 Central Assessment.** It is probably best to leave this until the last stage of your revision, and then attempt it as a 'mock' under 'exam conditions'. This will help you develop techniques in approaching the assessment and allocating time correctly. For further guidance on this, please see Central Assessment Technique on Page (xvii).

This approach is only a suggestion. You or your college may well adapt it to suit your needs.

Remember this is a **practical** course.

- Try to relate the material to your experience in the workplace or any other work experience you may have had.
- Try to make as many links as you can to your study of the other units at this level.

Lecturers' Resource Pack activities

At the back of this Kit we have included a number of chapter-linked activities without answers. We have also included a practice devolved assessment and a practice central assessment without answers. The answers for this section are in the BPP Lecturers' Resource Pack for this Unit.

Stop press

The AAT is planning to change the terminology used for assessments in the following ways:

(a) Central assessments to be called exam based testing
(b) Devolved assessments to be called skills based testing

As the plans had not been finalised at the time of going to press, the 2002 editions of BPP titles will continue to refer to central and devolved assessments.

UNIT 6 STANDARDS OF COMPETENCE

The structure of the Standards for Unit 6

The unit commences with a statement of the **knowledge and understanding** which underpin competence in the Unit's elements.

The unit is then divided into **elements of competence** describing activities which the individual should be able to perform.

Each element includes:

(a) A set of **performance criteria** which define what constitutes competent performance

(b) A **range statement** which defines the situations, contexts, methods etc in which competence should be displayed

(c) **Evidence requirements**, which state that competence must be demonstrated consistently, over an appropriate time scale with evidence of performance being provided from the appropriate sources

(d) **Sources of evidence**, being suggestions of ways in which you can find evidence to demonstrate that competence

The elements of competence for Unit 6 *Recording Cost Information* are set out below. Knowledge and understanding required for the unit as a whole are listed first, followed by the performance criteria, and range statements for each element. Performance criteria are cross-referenced below to chapters in the Unit 6 *Cost Information* Interactive Text.

Unit 6 Recording Cost Information

What is the unit about?

This unit is concerned with recording, analysing and reporting information relating to both direct and indirect costs. It involves the identification, coding and analysis of all costs, the apportionment and absorption of indirect costs and the presentation of all the information in standard cost reports. The candidate is required to carry out variance analyses, different methods of allocation, apportionment and absorption and adjustments for under/over recovered indirect costs. There is also a requirement for information to be systematically checked and any unusual or unexpected results to be communicated to management.

Knowledge and understanding

The business environment

- Main types of materials: raw materials; part finished goods; materials issued from stores within the organisation; deliveries (Elements 6.1 & 6.2)
- Methods of payment for labour: salaried labour; performance related pay; profit related pay (Elements 6.1 & 6.2)
- Main types of expenses: expenses directly charged to cost units; indirect expenses; depreciation charges (Elements 6.1 & 6.2)

Accounting techniques

- Basic analysis of variances: usage; price; rate; efficiency; expenditure; volume; capacity (Elements 6.1, 6.2 & 6.3)
- Procedures for establishing standard materials costs, use of technical and purchasing information (Element 6.1)
- Methods of analysing materials usage: reasons for wastage (Element 6.1)
- Procedures for establishing standard labour costs: use of information about labour rates (Element 6.1)
- Analysis of labour rate and efficiency: idle time; overtime levels; absenteeism; sickness rates (Element 6.1)
- Methods of stock control (Element 6.1)
- Methods of setting standards for expenses (Elements 6.1 & 6.2)
- Procedures and documentation relating to expenses (Elements 6.1 & 6.2)
- Allocation of expenses to cost centres (Elements 6.1 & 6.2)
- Analysis of the effect of changing activity levels on unit costs (Elements 6.1 & 6.2)
- Procedures for establishing standard absorption rates (Element 6.2)
- Bases of allocating and apportioning indirect costs to responsibility centres: direct; reciprocal allocation; step down method (Element 6.2)
- Activity based systems of allocating costs: cost drivers; cost pools (Element 6.2)
- Bases of absorption (Element 6.2)
- Methods of presenting information orally and in written reports (Element 6.3)
- Control ratios of efficiency, capacity and activity (Element 6.3)

Accounting principles and theory

- Relationship between technical systems and costing systems - job, batch, unit, systems (Elements 6.1 & 6.2)
- Principles and objectives of standard costing systems: variance reports (Elements 6.1, 6.2 & 6.3)
- Relationships between the materials costing system and the stock control system (Element 6.1)
- Relationships between the labour costing system and the payroll accounting system (Element 6.1)
- Relationships between the expenses costing system and the accounting system (Elements 6.1 & 6.2)

- Objectives of depreciation accounting (Elements 6.1 & 6.2)
- The distinction between fixed, semi-fixed and variable costs (Elements 6.1 & 6.2)
- Effect of changes in capacity levels (Element 6.2)
- Arbitrary nature of overhead apportionments (Element 6.2)
- The significance of and possible reasons for variances (Elements 6.1, 6.2 & 6.3)

The organisation

- Understanding of the ways the accounting systems of an organisation are affected by its organisational structure, its administrative systems and procedures and the nature of its business transactions (Elements 6.1, 6.2 & 6.3)
- The reporting cycle of the organisation (Element 6.3)

Element 6.1 Record and analyse information relating to direct costs

	Performance criteria	Chapters in Text
1	Direct costs are identified in accordance with the organisation's costing procedures	2-4,9
2	Information relating to direct costs is clearly and correctly coded, analysed and recorded	2-4, 7-9
3	Direct costs are calculated in accordance with the organisation's policies and procedures	2-4, 9
4	Standard costs are compared against actual costs and any variances are analysed	10, 11
5	Information is systematically checked against the overall usage and stock control practices	2
6	Queries are either resolved or referred to the appropriate person	2-4, 7

Range statement

1 Direct costs: standard and actual material costs; standard and actual labour costs; standard and actual expenses

- Materials: raw materials; part finished goods; materials issued from stores within the organisation; deliveries
- Labour: employees of the organisation on the payroll; sub-contractors; agency staff
- Expenses: direct revenue expenditure

2 Variance analysis: Materials variances: usage, price; Labour variances: rate, efficiency

Element 6.2 Record and analyse information relating to the allocation, apportionment and absorption of overhead costs

	Performance criteria	Chapters in Text
1	Data are correctly coded, analysed and recorded	2-4, 7
2	Overhead costs are established in accordance with the organisation's procedures	2-4, 9
3	Information relating to overhead costs is accurately and clearly recorded	2-4, 7-9
4	Overhead costs are correctly attributed to producing and service cost centres in accordance with agreed methods of allocation, apportionment and absorption	5
5	Adjustments for under or over recovered overhead costs are made in accordance with established procedures	5
6	Standard costs are compared against actual costs and any variances are analysed	10, 11
7	Methods of allocation, apportionment and absorption are reviewed at regular intervals in discussions with senior staff, and agreed changes to methods are implemented	5
8	Staff working in operational departments are consulted to resolve any queries in the data	2-4, 7

Range statement

1. Overhead costs: standard and actual indirect material costs; standard and actual indirect labour costs; indirect expenses; depreciation charges
2. Methods of allocation and apportionment: direct; reciprocal allocation; step down method
3. Variance analysis: Overhead variances: expenditure, efficiency, volume, capacity; Fixed overhead variances: expenditure, volume, capacity, efficiency

BPP PUBLISHING

Element 6.3 Prepare and present standard cost reports

	Performance criteria	**Chapters in Text**
1	Standard cost reports with variances clearly identified are presented in an intelligible form	11
2	Unusual or unexpected results are identified and reported to managers	11
3	Any reasons for significant variances from standard are identified and the explanations presented to management	11
4	The results of the analysis and explanations of specific variances are produced for management	11
5	Staff working in operational departments are consulted to resolve any queries in the data	11
	Range statement	
1	Methods of presentation: written report containing analysis and explanation of specific variances; further explanations to managers	
2	Types of variances: Overhead variances: expenditure, efficiency, volume, capacity; Materials variances: usage, price; Labour variances: rate, efficiency	

ASSESSMENT STRATEGY

This unit is assessed by both **central assessment/exam based testing** and by **devolved assessment/skills based testing.**

CENTRAL ASSESSMENT

A central assessment is a means of collecting evidence that you have the **essential knowledge and understanding** which underpins competence. It is also a means of collecting evidence across the **range of contexts** for the standards, and of assessing your ability to **transfer skills**, knowledge and understanding to different situations. Thus, although central assessments contain practical tests linked to the performance criteria, they also focus on the underpinning knowledge and understanding. You should in addition expect each central assessment to contain tasks taken from across a broad range of the standards.

CENTRAL ASSESSMENT TECHNIQUE

Completing central assessments successfully at this level is half about having the knowledge, and half about doing yourself full justice on the day. You must have the right **technique**.

The day of the central assessment

1 Set at least one **alarm** (or get an alarm call) for a morning central assessment.

2 Have **something to eat** but beware of eating too much; you may feel sleepy if your system is digesting a large meal.

3 Allow plenty of **time to get to where you are sitting the central assessment**; have your route worked out in advance and listen to news bulletins to check for potential travel problems.

4 **Don't forget** pens, pencils, rulers, erasers.

5 Put **new batteries** into your calculator and take a spare set (or a spare calculator).

6 **Avoid discussion** about the central assessment with other candidates outside the venue.

Technique in the central assessment

1 ***Read the instructions (the 'rubric') on the front of the assessment carefully***

Check that the format hasn't changed. It is surprising how often assessors' reports remark on the number of students who do not attempt all the tasks.

2 ***Read the paper twice***

Read through the paper once - don't forget that you are given 15 minutes' reading time - then quickly jot down key points against each task in a second read through. Check carefully that you have got the right end of the stick before putting pen to paper. Use your 15 minutes' reading time wisely.

3 *Check the time allocation for each section of the assessment*

Time allocations are given for each section of the assessment. When the time for a section is up, you should go on to the next section.

4 *Read the task carefully and plan your answer*

Read through the task again very carefully when you come to answer it. Plan your answer to ensure that you **keep to the point**. Two minutes of planning plus eight minutes of writing is virtually certain to produce a better answer than ten minutes of writing. Planning will also help you answer the assessment efficiently, for example by identifying workings that can be used for more than one task.

5 *Produce relevant answers*

Particularly with written answers, make sure you **answer what has been set**, and not what you would have preferred to have been set. Do not for example answer a question on **why** something is done with an explanation of **how** it is done.

6 *Work your way steadily through the assessment*

Don't get bogged down in one task. If you are having problems with something, the chances are that everyone else is too.

7 *Produce an answer in the correct format*

The assessor will state **in the requirements** the format which should be used, for example in a report or memorandum.

8 *Do what the assessor wants*

You should ask yourself what the assessor is expecting in an answer; many tasks will demand a combination of technical knowledge and business common-sense. Be careful if you are required to give a decision or make a recommendation; you cannot just list the criteria you will use, but you will also have to say whether those criteria have been fulfilled.

9 *Lay out your numerical computations and use workings correctly*

Make sure the layout is in a style the assessor likes.

Show all your **workings** clearly and explain what they mean. Cross reference them to your answer. This will help the assessor to follow your method (this is of particular importance where there may be several possible answers).

10 *Present a tidy paper*

You are a professional, and it should show in the **presentation of your work**. You should make sure that you write legibly, label diagrams clearly and lay out your work neatly.

11 *Stay until the end of the central assessment*

Use any spare time **checking and rechecking** your script. Check that you have answered all the requirements of the task and that you have clearly labelled your work. Consider also whether your answer appears reasonable in the light of the information given in the question.

12 *Don't worry if you feel you have performed badly in the central assessment*

It is more than likely that the other candidates will have found the assessment difficult too. As soon as you get up to leave the venue, **forget** that central assessment and think about the next - or, if it is the last one, celebrate!

13 ***Don't discuss a central assessment with other candidates***

This is particularly the case if you **still have other central assessments to sit**. Even if you have finished, you should put it out of your mind until the day of the results. Forget about assessments and relax!

DEVOLVED ASSESSMENT

Devolved assessment is a means of collecting evidence of your ability to carry out **practical activities** and to **operate effectively in the conditions of the workplace** to the standards required. Evidence may be collected at your place of work or at an Approved Assessment Centre by means of simulations of workplace activity, or by a combination of these methods.

If the Approved Assessment Centre is a **workplace**, you may be observed carrying out accounting activities as part of your normal work routine. You should collect documentary evidence of the work you have done, or contributed to, in an **accounting portfolio**. Evidence collected in a portfolio can be assessed in addition to observed performance or where it is not possible to assess by observation.

Where the Approved Assessment Centre is a **college or training organisation**, devolved assessment will be by means of a combination of the following.

- Documentary evidence of activities carried out at the workplace, collected by you in an **accounting portfolio.**
- Realistic **simulations** of workplace activities. These simulations may take the form of case studies and in-tray exercises and involve the use of primary documents and reference sources.
- **Projects and assignments** designed to assess the Standards of Competence.

If you are unable to provide workplace evidence you will be able to complete the assessment requirements by the alternative methods listed above.

Possible assessment methods

Where possible, evidence should be collected in the workplace, but this may not be a practical prospect for you. Equally, where workplace evidence can be gathered it may not cover all elements. The AAT regards performance evidence from simulations, case studies, projects and assignments as an acceptable substitute for performance at work, provided that they are based on the Standards and, as far as possible, on workplace practice.

There are a number of methods of assessing accounting competence. The list below is not exhaustive, nor is it prescriptive. Some methods have limited applicability, but others are capable of being expanded to provide challenging tests of competence.

Assessment method	Suitable for assessing
Performance of an accounting task either in the workplace or by simulation: eg preparing and processing documents, posting entries, making adjustments, balancing, calculating, analysing information etc by manual or computerised processes	**Basic task competence.** Adding supplementary oral questioning may help to draw out underpinning knowledge and understanding and highlight your ability to deal with contingencies and unexpected occurrences
General case studies. These are broader than simulations. They include more background information about the system and business environment	Ability to **analyse a system** and suggest ways of modifying it. It could take the form of a written report, with or without the addition of oral or written questions
Accounting problems/cases: eg a list of balances that require adjustments and the preparation of final accounts	Understanding of the **general principles of accounting** as applied to a particular case or topic
Preparation of flowcharts/diagrams. To illustrate an actual (or simulated) accounting procedure	**Understanding of the logic** behind a procedure, of controls, and of relationships between departments and procedures. Questions on the flow chart or diagram can provide evidence of underpinning knowledge and understanding
Interpretation of accounting information from an actual or simulated situation. The assessment could include non-financial information and written or oral questioning	**Interpretative competence**
Preparation of written reports on an actual or simulated situation	**Written communication skills**
Analysis of critical incidents, problems encountered, achievements	Your ability to handle **contingencies**
Listing of likely errors eg preparing a list of the main types of errors likely to occur in an actual or simulated procedure	Appreciation of the range of **contingencies** likely to be encountered. Oral or written questioning would be a useful supplement to the list
Outlining the organisation's policies, guidelines and regulations	Performance criteria relating to these aspects of competence. It also provides evidence of competence in **researching information**
Objective tests and short-answer questions	**Specific knowledge**
In-tray exercises	Your **task-management ability** as well as technical competence

Assessment method	Suitable for assessing
Supervisors' reports	**General job competence**, personal effectiveness, reliability, accuracy, and time management. Reports need to be related specifically to the Standards of Competence
Analysis of work logbooks/diaries	**Personal effectiveness**, time management etc. It may usefully be supplemented with oral questioning
Formal written answers to questions	Knowledge and understanding of the **general accounting environment** and its impact on particular units of competence.
Oral questioning	**Knowledge and understanding** across the range of competence including organisational procedures, methods of dealing with unusual cases, contingencies and so on. It is often used in conjunction with other methods.

BUILDING YOUR PORTFOLIO

What is a portfolio?

A portfolio is a collection of work that demonstrates what the owner can do. In AAT language the portfolio demonstrates **competence**.

A painter will have a collection of his paintings to exhibit in a gallery, an advertising executive will have a range of advertisements and ideas that she has produced to show to a prospective client. Both the collection of paintings and the advertisements form the portfolio of that artist or advertising executive.

Your portfolio will be unique to you just as the portfolio of the artist will be unique because no one will paint the same range of pictures in the same way. It is a very personal collection of your work and should be treated as a **confidential** record.

What evidence should a portfolio include?

No two portfolios will be the same but by following some simple guidelines you can decide which of the following suggestions will be appropriate in your case.

(a) **Your current CV**

This should be at the front. It will give your personal details as well as brief descriptions of posts you have held with the most recent one shown first.

(b) **References and testimonials**

References from previous employers may be included especially those of which you are particularly proud.

(c) **Your current job description**

You should emphasise financial **responsibilities and duties.**

(d) **Your student record sheets**

These should be supplied by AAT when you begin your studies, and your training provider should also have some if necessary.

(e) **Evidence from your current workplace**

This could take many forms including **letters, memos, reports** you have written, **copies of accounts** or **reconciliations** you have prepared, **discrepancies** you have investigated etc. Remember to obtain permission to include the evidence from your line manager because some records may be sensitive. Discuss the performance criteria that are listed in your Student Record Sheets with your training provider and employer, and think of other evidence that could be appropriate to you.

(f) **Evidence from your social activities**

For example you may be the treasurer of a club in which case examples of your cash and banking records could be appropriate.

(g) **Evidence from your studies**

Few students are able to satisfy all the requirements of competence by workplace evidence alone. They therefore rely on simulations to provide the remaining evidence to complete a unit. If you are not working or not working in a relevant post, then you may need to rely more heavily on simulations as a source of evidence.

(h) **Additional work**

Your training provider may give you work that specifically targets one or a group of performance criteria in order to complete a unit. It could take the form of questions, presentations or demonstrations. Each training provider will approach this in a different way.

(i) **Evidence from a previous workplace**

This evidence may be difficult to obtain and should be used with caution because it must satisfy the 'rules' of evidence, that is it must be current. Only rely on this as evidence if you have changed jobs recently.

(j) **Prior achievements**

For example you may have already completed the health and safety unit during a previous course of study, and therefore there is no need to repeat this work. Advise your training provider who will check to ensure that it is the same unit and record it as complete if appropriate.

How should it be presented?

As you assemble the evidence remember to **make a note** of it on your Student Record Sheet in the space provided and **cross reference** it. In this way it is easy to check to see if your evidence is **appropriate**. Remember one piece of evidence may satisfy a number of performance criteria so remember to check this thoroughly and discuss it with your training provider if in doubt.

To keep all your evidence together a ring binder or lever arch file is a good means of storage.

When should evidence be assembled?

You should begin to assemble evidence **as soon as you have registered as a student**. **Don't leave it all** until the last few weeks of your studies, because you may miss vital deadlines and your resulting certificate sent by the AAT may not include all the units you have completed. Give yourself and your training provider time to examine your portfolio and report your results to AAT at regular intervals. In this way the task of assembling the portfolio will be spread out over a longer period of time and will be presented in a more professional manner.

What are the key criteria that the portfolio must fulfil?

As you assemble your evidence bear in mind that it must be:

- **Valid**. It must relate to the Standards.
- **Authentic**. It must be your own work.
- **Current**. It must refer to your current or most recent job.
- **Sufficient**. It must meet all the performance criteria by the time you have completed your portfolio.

What are the most important elements in a portfolio that covers Unit 6?

You should remember that the unit is about **recording cost information**. Therefore you need to produce evidence not only demonstrating that you can carry out certain tasks, but also you must show that you can record cost information correctly.

For Element 6.1 *Record and analyse information relating to direct costs*, you not only need to show that you can identify which costs in your organisation are direct, you also need to demonstrate that you can code them correctly and calculate any direct variances which have arisen.

The main evidence that you need for Element 6.2 *Record and analyse information relating to the allocation, apportionment and absorption of overhead costs* is detail of how overheads are correctly allocated, apportioned and absorbed in accordance with your organisation's procedures. You will also need to demonstrate that you have calculated overhead variances and analysed any which are significant.

To fulfil the requirements of Element 6.3 *Prepare and present standard cost reports* you need to demonstrate that you have calculated and analysed material, labour and overhead variances and presented them to management. You will also need to provide evidence of the methods of presentation that you have used in order to communicate this information (for example, written reports).

Finally

Remember that the portfolio is **your property** and **your responsibility**. Not only could it be presented to the external verifier before your award can be confirmed; it could be used when you are seeking **promotion** or applying for a more senior and better paid post elsewhere. How your portfolio is presented can say as much about you as the evidence inside.

Practice activities

1 Cost information

1 MIXED FARM — Pre-assessment

For a mixed farm, growing crops and raising cattle, suggest one cost unit and two cost centres.

2 INDIRECT MATERIALS — Pre-assessment

Indirect materials costs can also be called indirect expenses. True or false?

3 ADVANTAGE — Assessment

What is the advantage of charging as many costs as possible to cost units rather than treating them as overheads?

4 COST UNITS — Assessment

Suggest the cost units which would be appropriate for management information systems in the following industries.

(a) A building contractor
(b) An airline

2 Materials

5 REORDER LEVELS — Assessment

A company has established reorder levels for each of the major materials it holds. Give *two* factors which influence a reorder level.

6 STOCK LEVELS — Assessment

Explain briefly the purpose of establishing minimum stock levels for each type of material in a stock control system.

7 REQUISITION — Pre-assessment

What is the purpose of:

(a) a materials requisition?
(b) a purchase requisition?

8 ANNUAL DEMAND — Assessment

Annual demand for a material is 200,000 units. It costs £3.20 to hold one unit in stock for one year. Ordering costs are £18 per order. What should the reorder quantity be in order to minimise the costs of holding and ordering stock?

9 FIFO TO LIFO — Assessment

At a time of rapidly rising prices a manufacturing company decides to change from a FIFO to a LIFO system of pricing material issues. What would be the effect on the following?

(a) Stock valuation
(b) Cost of materials charged to production

10 OPTIMUM LEVEL — Assessment

Give four factors which should be considered in deciding the optimum level of stocks of component parts to be held in a stores which serves a mass production assembly line.

11 MAXIMUM LEVEL — Assessment

On what factors does a maximum stock level depend?

3 Labour

12 DIFFERENTIAL PIECEWORK — Assessment

What is differential piecework?

13 EMPLOYEES — Assessment

List two advantages of paying employees by the results achieved.

14 HOURLY RATES — Assessment

Give two reasons why the majority of employees are paid on the basis of time, eg hourly rates of pay.

15 WEEKEND WORKING — Assessment

How would additional payments to production workers for weekend working be treated in the cost accounts?

4 Expenses

16 PERSONAL COMPUTER **Assessment**

A personal computer costing £3,000 was expected to last for four years and to have a resale value of £200 at the end of this period. The company policy is to depreciate assets using the straight-line method of depreciation.

(a) What is the annual depreciation charge to the administration cost centre?

(b) The computer was replaced after three years with no resale value. Calculate the obsolescence charge and state where this charge should be shown in the cost accounts.

5 Overheads and absorption costing

17 OVERHEAD COSTS — Pre-assessment

Give two significant overhead costs likely to be incurred by an international firm of management consultants.

18 ACTUAL OVERHEADS — Assessment

The actual overheads for a department were £6,500 last period and the actual output was 540 machine hours. The budgeted overheads were £5,995 and the budgeted output was 550 machine hours. Calculate the under- or over-absorbed overhead and state whether it would increase or reduce the profit for the period.

19 COST DRIVERS — Assessment

With activity based costing, 'cost drivers' are used.

(a) Are cost drivers a means of:

(i) establishing the overhead cost of activities; or
(ii) calculating the value of the direct materials used; or
(iii) determining the most suitable cost centres.

(b) Suggest a suitable cost driver for the purchasing department of a large manufacturing company.

20 MACHINING DEPARTMENT — Pre-assessment

The overhead absorption rate for the machining department at Jefferson Ltd is £5 per direct labour hour. During the year to 31 December 1,753 direct labour hours were worked and overheads incurred were £9,322. During the twelve-month period overheads were therefore over absorbed. True or false?

21 MACHINE HOUR RATE METHOD — Assessment

Explain briefly the machine hour rate method of absorbing overhead costs into cost units in a manufacturing organisation.

22 ABC — Assessment

Explain briefly the function of cost drivers in an activity based costing system, giving an example.

23 LABOUR INTENSIVE — Assessment

When using absorption costing, explain why the use of an overhead absorption rate based on direct labour hours is generally favoured over a direct wages percentage rate for a labour intensive operation.

6 Cost behaviour

24 COST BEHAVIOUR PATTERNS — Assessment

Draw graphs to illustrate the following cost behaviour patterns.

(a) Variable cost
(b) Fixed cost
(c) Step cost

25 LAKE GARDA LTD — Assessment

The costs of operating the stores department of Lake Garda Ltd for the last four years have been as follows.

Year	*Output volume*	*Total cost*
	units	£
1	70,000	1,100,000
2	80,000	1,150,000
3	77,000	1,110,000
4	60,000	970,000

Task

What costs should be expected in year 5 when output is expected to be 75,000 units?

7 Bookkeeping entries for cost information

26 FRATERNITY LTD — Assessment

Fraternity Ltd manufactures a range of products which are sold through a network of wholesalers and dealers. A set of integrated accounts is kept, and for the year 20X0 the following information is relevant.

(a) Production overhead is absorbed into the cost of products on the basis of a budgeted rate of 80% of direct labour cost.

(b) Finished stocks are valued at factory cost.

(c)

	31 March 20X0	*30 April 20X0*
	£	£
Raw materials stock	34,400	30,320
Work in progress stock	11,200	9,500
Finished goods stock	21,000	24,180
Debtors for goods sold	18,400	22,280
Creditors for raw materials	15,200	18,840
Fixed assets at net book value	12,000	11,600

(d) Bank transactions for the month of April 20X0 were as follows.

	£
Bank balance at 31 March	3,000
Receipts from debtors	55,120
Payments made	
Direct labour	12,800
Creditors for raw materials	17,920
Production overhead	10,400
Administration overhead	1,400
Selling and distribution overhead	4,600

(e) Production overhead includes a monthly charge of £400 for depreciation and the opening balance on the production overhead control account each month is nil. Administration, selling and distribution overheads consist entirely of cash items.

Task

Use the information above to prepare the following control accounts.

(a) Raw materials stock
(b) Work in progress stock
(c) Finished goods stock
(d) Production overhead

8 Costing methods

27 BATCH COSTING **Pre-assessment**

Fill in the missing words.

Batch costing is a form of costing that is similar to______________costing except that costs are collected for______________. The cost unit is the____________. A cost per unit is calculated by____________________________________.

28 COSTING METHODS **Assessment**

Suggest appropriate costing methods for the following organisations.

(a) A plumbing business
(b) A clothing manufacturer
(c) A caterer

9 *Standard costing*

29 STANDARD TIME — Assessment

An employee makes 200 units of product A, 350 units of product B and 300 units of product C. The standard time allowed per unit was:

A 4 minutes B 2 minutes C 3 minutes

Calculate the standard hours produced by the employee.

30 STANDARD COST — Pre-assessment

A standard cost is only a guess at what the cost of something should be. It is of little relevance once the actual cost is known. True or false?

31 IDEAL STANDARD — Assessment

Name one advantage and one disadvantage of using an ideal standard.

10 Calculation of variances

32 CASIOS LTD — Assessment

Choose the appropriate words.

The workforce of Casios Ltd has been working at a less efficient rate than standard to produce a given output. The result is a favourable/adverse fixed overhead efficiency/capacity variance.

The total number of hours worked was, however, more than originally budgeted. The effect is measured by a favourable/adverse fixed overhead efficiency/capacity variance.

33 VARIANCE — Assessment

How is a usage or efficiency variance calculated?

34 BRYAN LIMITED — Assessment

Bryan Limited budgets to produce 500 units of ferginude during August 20X2. The expected time to produce one unit of ferginude is 2.5 hours and the budgeted fixed production overhead is £10,000. Actual fixed production overhead expenditure in August 20X2 turns out to be £10,500 and the labour force manages to produce 600 units in 1,350 hours of work.

Comment on the above information, performing whatever calculations you think are most appropriate.

35 RESPONSIBILITY — Assessment

(a) Who is likely to be responsible for an adverse **material usage variance**?

(b) Who is likely to be responsible for an adverse **labour rate variance**?

11 Further aspects of variance analysis

36 BEST METHOD — Assessment

A direct material price variance may be calculated and entered in the accounts of a business at either the time of receipt of the stock, or the time of issue from stores to production. Which of the methods is usually regarded as the better, and why?

37 EXCELSIOR PLC — Assessment

In a particular month production overheads were under absorbed because Excelsior plc had to cut back production due to a lack of orders.

(a) Which variance account would be affected by this situation?

(b) What would be the effect on unit costs of production?

38 INTERDEPENDENCE — Assessment

Explain the meaning of the term 'interdependence of variances'.

39 JEMIMA LTD — Assessment

Jemima Ltd uses a standard costing system and values all of its stocks of raw materials at standard price. Stocks are issued to work in progress at standard price. There is an adverse material price variance during an accounting period. What is the cost accounting entry for the material price variance?

General activities

The following practice activities cover topics relating to more than one chapter in the **Cost Information** Interactive Text.

The following data relate to practice activities 40-42.

RFB plc was formed in the early nineteenth century producing wheels for horse-drawn vehicles. Today it is a successful, profitable company which still makes wheels, but for a variety of uses: wheelbarrows, carts, toys etc. The production operation consists of three departments: bending, cutting and assembly. The bending and cutting departments have general purpose machinery which is used to manufacture all the wheels produced.

40 ANALYSIS **Assessment**

Complete the form below by analysing the cost items into the appropriate columns and agreeing the balances.

	Total £	*Prime cost* £	*Production expense* £	*Admin. expense* £	*Selling and distribution expense* £
Wages of assembly employees	6,750				
Wages of stores employees	3,250				
Tyres for toy wheels	1,420				
Safety goggles for operators	810				
Job advert for new employees	84				
Depreciation of delivery vehicles	125				
Depreciation of production machines	264				
Cost of trade exhibition	1,200				
Computer stationery	130				
Course fee for AAT training	295				
Royalty for the design of wheel 1477	240				
	14,568				

41 PURCHASE INVOICES **Assessment**

Extracts from three purchase invoices which have been received for wire, code number 1471 are shown as follows. The invoices have been passed by the purchase department and the standard price is £120 per coil.

(a) (i) Calculate the standard cost of the actual quantity purchased on each invoice.

(ii) Name and calculate the variance, stating whether it is adverse or favourable, in each invoice.

Invoice number 3275	Your order number 57623
Date 1.11.X8	£
50 coils @ £132	6,600
Standard cost of actual quantity	______
.... variance	______( )

Invoice number 4517	Your order number 58127
Date 17.11.X8	£
150 coils @ £108	16,200
Standard cost of actual quantity	______
.... variance	______( )

Invoice number 5178	Your order number 60173
Date 17.11.X8	£
100 coils @ £120	12,000
Standard cost of actual quantity	______
.... variance	______( )

(b) Enter the individual variances calculated in (a) in the variance account below. Do not calculate the balance on the account.

VARIANCE ACCOUNT

(c) Suggest reasons for the variances in (a), and state what action, if any, needs to be taken. Who would be responsible for taking the action that you recommend?

42 PROTECTIVE GLOVES **Assessment**

Protective gloves are used in the production departments and are drawn from stores at regular intervals. Records show the following for November:

1.11.X8	Opening stock	100 pairs @ £2 each
7.11.X8	Purchases	200 pairs @ £1.90 each
18.11.X8	Issues	150 pairs

Calculate the value of the closing stock of gloves given that the FIFO system of valuing issues is used.

The following data relate to practice activities 43-44.

AMP plc, a printing company, specialises in producing accounting manuals for several accountancy training companies. The manuals are written by the training companies and passed to AMP. The company uses three main stages in producing the manuals:

(a) The preparation of the text
(b) The printing of the text
(c) The assembly and binding of the manuals

43 STORES RECORD CARD **Assessment**

Write up the following information on the stores record card given below using weighted average prices to value the issues.

Material: Paper - Code 1564A
Opening stock: 10,000 sheets - value £3,000

Purchases			*Issues*	
3 May	4,000 sheets	£1,600	6 May	7,000 sheets
12 May	10,000 sheets	£3,100	15 May	6,000 sheets
25 May	10,000 sheets	£3,200	22 May	7,200 sheets

(The calculation of the weighted average should be to two decimal places of a £ and that of the value of the issues to the nearest £.)

Stores Record Card

Material: Paper *Code:* 1564A

Date	Details	*Receipts*		*Issues*			*Stock*		
		Sheets	£	*Sheets*	*Price*	£	*Sheets*	*Price*	£

44 PAPER **Pre-assessment**

AMP has always held large quantities of paper in stock in case it should become difficult to obtain. Suggest two problems that this could create.

The following data relate to practice activities 45-49.

Pears plc manufactures children's clothing. The general manager is concerned about how the costs of the various garments it produces are calculated. The material cost varies from one garment to another and the rates of pay in the various departments also vary to reflect the different skills offered. Both these prime costs are charged direct to individual garments so that any variation is taken into account. It is the overhead cost which has been concerning Pears for some time. The present overhead system uses one overhead rate for the whole company and is absorbed as a percentage of direct labour cost. The accounting department has been examining individual cost items and relating them as closely as possible to the department which incurs them. Some apportionment has also taken place and the forecasted overhead cost and other related information is as follows.

	Overhead cost £'000	*Numbers employed*	*% of floor area*	*Material issued* £'000	*Machine hours*
Production departments					
Cutting	187	10	40	200	15,000
Sewing	232	15	30	250	25,000
Finishing	106	8	15	100	
Service departments					
Stores	28	2	5	-	
Maintenance	50	3	10	50	

45 OVERHEAD ANALYSIS SHEET **Assessment**

Using the overhead analysis sheet below, apportion:

(a) The stores department's costs to the production and maintenance departments;

(b) The maintenance department's costs to the cutting and sewing departments only.

Select the most suitable base for each apportionment and state the bases used on the overhead analysis sheet. (Calculations should be to the nearest £.)

OVERHEAD ANALYSIS SHEET DATE

	TOTAL	PRODUCTION			SERVICE	
		Cutting	Sewing	Finishing	Stores	Maintenance
	£	£	£	£	£	£
Overheads	603,000	187,000	232,000	106,000	28,000	50,000
Apportion Stores (Base:)						
Apportion Maintenance (Base:)						

46 LABOUR HOURS **Assessment**

Given that 12,000 labour hours will be worked in the finishing department calculate overhead absorption rates for the three production departments using machine hour rates for the cutting and sewing departments, and a labour hour rate for the finishing department. (Calculations should be to two decimal places of the £.)

47 MACHINE HOUR RATES **Assessment**

Explain briefly why it is appropriate to use machine hour rates in the cutting and sewing departments.

48 XL **Assessment**

Using the form provided below, calculate the standard cost of a new garment 'XL'. It is established that direct material cost will be £4.32. Direct labour cost is to be based on ¼ hour in the cutting department, 1 hour in the sewing department and ½ hour in the finishing department. The standard hourly rates of pay are £8.00 in cutting, £6.00 in sewing and £10.00 in finishing. Overheads are to be included using the hourly rates calculated in Practice activity 46. The machine hours in the cutting and sewing departments are equal to the labour hours for this product.

STANDARD PRODUCT COST SHEET
PRODUCT : 'XL'

Date:

	Hours	Rate £	£	£
Direct Material Cost				
Direct Labour Cost				
- cutting				
- sewing				
- finishing				
Total Labour Cost				
Overhead Cost				
- cutting				
- sewing				
- finishing				
Total Overhead Cost				
TOTAL COST				

49 MATERIAL METRES **Assessment**

Pears plc has obtained 50 metres of a material at a special price of £2.00 per metre as it is slightly substandard. The standard price for this material is £3.00 per metre. From this material 20 garments have been made for which the standard quantity is 2 metres per garment.

(a) Calculate the following.

- (i) Material price variance
- (ii) Material usage variance
- (iii) Total material cost variance

(b) List the responsible managers who should be informed of the price and usage variances as part of the routine reporting procedures.

(c) Explain whether the decision to buy this material was correct.

The following data relate to practice activities 50-54.

(NB. Answer these activities in sequence as the answers to earlier activities may need to be used later.)

Watkins Ltd produces a single product, the N-17T, which passes through three production processes (forming, colouring and assembly). The output of the forming process becomes the input of the colouring process and the input of the assembly process is the output of the colouring process. There are also two service departments, maintenance and general.

The budgeted overheads for the 12 months to 31 December 20X9 are as follows.

	£	£
Rent and rates		8,000
Power		750
Light, heat		5,000
Repairs, maintenance:		
Forming	800	
Colouring	1,800	
Assembly	300	
Maintenance	200	
General	100	
		3,200
Departmental expenses:		
Forming	1,500	
Colouring	2,300	
Assembly	1,100	
Maintenance	900	
General	1,500	
		7,300
Depreciation:		
Plant		10,000
Fixtures and fittings		250
Insurance:		
Plant		2,000
Buildings		500
Indirect labour:		
Forming	3,000	
Colouring	5,000	
Assembly	1,500	
Maintenance	4,000	
General	2,000	
		15,500
		52,500

Other data are available as follows.

	Floor area	*Plant value*	*Fixtures & fittings*	*Horse-power*	*Effective labour hours*	*Budget machine hours*
	m^2	£	£			
Forming	2,000	25,000	1,000	40	27,400	5,000
Colouring	4,000	60,000	500	90	3,000	14,400
Assembly	3,000	7,500	2,000	15	20,000	2,600
Maintenance	500	7,500	1,000	5	-	-
General	500	-	500	-	-	-
	10,000	100,000	5,000	150	50,400	22,000

	Budget	
	Maintenance work to be provided by maintenance department	*General work to be provided by general service department*
	Hours	Hours
Forming	2,000	1,200
Colouring	5,000	3,600
Assembly	2,000	600
Maintenance	-	600
General	1,000	-
	10,000	6,000

50 TABLE START **Assessment**

Prepare a table which shows the overheads which can be directly allocated to the five departments.

51 TABLE FINISH **Assessment**

Complete the table you started in Practice activity 50 by apportioning the remaining overheads to the five departments, clearly indicating the basis of apportionment that you have used.

52 REPEATED DISTRIBUTION METHOD **Assessment**

Apportion the service department overheads to the production departments using the repeated distribution method.

53 THREE DEPARTMENTS **Assessment**

Calculate suitable overhead absorption rates for the three production departments.

54 DECEMBER 20X9 **Assessment**

During the year to 31 December 20X9, 30,000 labour hours were worked in the forming department, 3,150 in the colouring department and 18,500 in the assembly department. Machines ran for 4,900 hours in the forming department, 16,000 hours in the colouring department and 3,297 in the assembly department. The overheads actually incurred in the three production departments (after allocation and apportionment) were as follows.

	£
Forming	14,580
Colouring	30,050
Assembly	9,840

Calculate any under- or over-absorbed overhead for the twelve months to 31 December 20X9.

The following data relate to practice activities 55 and 56.

Poltimore plc operates a job costing system which is fully integrated with the financial accounts.

55 POLTIMORE PLC — Assessment

On 1 May 20X9, there was only one uncompleted job in Poltimore plc's factory. The job card for this work is summarised below.

JOB CARD

Job 212/A

Costs to date	£
Direct materials	7,080
Direct labour	1,314
Production overhead	2,628
Factory cost to date	11,022

During May a number of new jobs were started. The chief cost accountant is exceptionally busy and so you have been asked to prepare job accounts for jobs 212/A and one of the new jobs, 219/C. Both jobs were completed during May. You have gathered together the following information.

	Direct materials	£
Issued to	212/A	3,122
	219/C	4,003
Transfers from	212/A to 219/C	3,500
Direct labour		
	212/A	1,922
	219/C	7,255

Prepare job accounts for 212/A and 219/C

56 PROFIT OR LOSS — Assessment

If administration and marketing overheads are added to cost of sales at a rate of 15% of factory cost and invoiced amounts are £20,500 for job 212/A and £28,750 for job 219/C, calculate the profit or loss on the two jobs.

Practice devolved assessments

Practice devolved assessment 1 Strange (Properties) Ltd

Performance criteria

The following performance criteria are covered in this Practice devolved assessment.

Element 6.1: Record and analyse information relating to direct costs

1 Direct costs are identified in accordance with the organisation's costing procedures

2 Information relating to direct costs is clearly and correctly coded, analysed and recorded

3 Direct costs are calculated in accordance with the organisation's policies and procedures

6 Queries are either resolved or referred to the appropriate person

Element 6.2: Record and analyse information relating to the allocation, apportionment and absorption of overhead costs

1 Data are correctly coded, analysed and recorded

2 Overhead costs are established in accordance with the organisation's procedures

3 Information relating to overhead costs is accurately and clearly recorded

4 Overhead costs are correctly attributed to producing and service cost centres in accordance with agreed methods of allocation, apportionment and absorption

5 Adjustments for under or over recovered overhead costs are made in accordance with established procedures

7 Methods of allocation, apportionment and absorption are revised at regular intervals in discussions with senior staff and agreed changes to methods are implemented

8 Staff working in operational departments are consulted to resolve any queries in the data

Notes on completing the Assessment

This Assessment is designed to test your ability to operate and maintain a system of accounting for expenses and a system for the apportionment and absorption of indirect costs.

You are provided with data on Pages 27 to 38 which you must use to complete the tasks on Pages 35 and 38.

You are allowed **three hours** to complete your work.

A high level of accuracy is required. Check your work carefully.

Correcting fluid should not be used. Errors should be crossed out neatly and clearly. You should write in ink - not pencil.

A FULL SUGGESTED ANSWER TO THIS ASSESSMENT IS PROVIDED ON PAGE 183.

Do not turn to the suggested answer until you have completed all parts of the Assessment.

STRANGE (PROPERTIES) LTD

Data

Your name is John Vernon and you joined Strange (Properties) Ltd at the beginning of November, taking over as head of the accounts department on the retirement of Brian Dimple who had occupied the post for many years.

Strange (Properties) Ltd is a property management company headed by Edward Strange, a solicitor, and his brother Victor, a chartered surveyor. The company looks after all of the affairs of around thirty blocks of flats or estates in the surrounding area. This involves company secretarial services, conveyancing, dealing with disputes, regular inspections of sites, obtaining tenders for repairs and maintenance contracts, bookkeeping, cash management and so on - a huge variety of tasks in fact.

During your first month you have spent most of your time chasing debtors, since there are many long-outstanding debts and a large bank overdraft as a consequence. You have left the day to day cash management to your two assistants. However, you have just received the following memo and attachments from Edward Strange.

MEMO

To: John Vernon
From: Edward Strange
Date: 1 December 20X2
Subject: Charges to clients

A number of our clients have complained recently about the way our charges fluctuate from month to month. Have you seen this list that the auditors did for July to September? I vaguely remember that your predecessor, Brian Dimple, used to say something about costing, and things not balancing, and fictional whatnots, but this was in the days before we bought the computer. Perhaps things are different now.

I was talking to an accountant at the golf club the other night and he started on about various different sorts of costing. 'Standard costing' was mentioned and 'absorbent costing'. One I thought might be appropriate to Strange (Properties) was 'process costing': I've heard you talk about processing invoices and data processing and the like.

Could you have a think about this and let me have a suggestion. I'll grin and bear it if 'notional thingummies' really are too bothersome, but I would like to appease our uppity paymasters if it does no harm to our business.

Enc. List of client charges; letter to Loudwater Place, copy invoices.

Client charges
July to September 20X2

	July	*August*	*September*
	£	£	£
Ashby Mansions, Harlington	2,336	2,705	2,220
Burgess Court, Southall	2,580	3,425	2,716
Clerk Court, Ealing	3,112	2,913	2,580
Clift Flats, Heston	2,656	3,233	2,959
Clifton Gardens, Hounslow	2,761	2,705	2,875
Coomer Place, Putney	2,730	2,705	2,142
Davison Close, Acton	2,200	3,215	2,330
De Beauvoir Buildings, Chiswick	2,807	4,171	2,975
Endymion Place, Hammersmith	3,230	2,705	2,721
Frampton Court, Fulham	5,185	3,429	2,142
Gibbs House, Hounslow	2,586	2,847	2,850
Glebe Gardens, Perivale	2,200	2,705	2,455
Grasmere Mansion, Isleworth	2,943	3,131	2,142
Hennigan House, Wembley	2,544	3,482	2,562
Jones Court, Fulham	2,338	2,705	5,740
Ketley Close, Sheen	6,905	2,705	3,909
Kings Buildings, Petersham	2,596	2,962	2,462
Laine House, Hanwell	2,806	2,765	2,804
Loudwater Place, Kew	2,200	8,983	3,858
Matkins Gardens, Hounslow	2,751	2,910	2,142
Mallow Close, Ealing	2,531	3,554	2,458
Neville House, Acton	3,463	2,961	2,791
Oakwood Buildings, Roehampton	2,580	2,864	2,304
Queen's Court, Isleworth	2,479	2,705	3,102
Rhodes Close, Sheen	3,177	3,655	2,142
Rodway House, Chiswick	2,200	3,023	2,284
Seymour Manor, Hammersmith	2,891	2,705	2,538
Tilbury Tower, Wembley	3,448	2,846	2,403
Undercliff Gardens, Richmond	2,652	2,917	3,392
Wyndham Rise, Southall	2,549	3,454	2,142

Wyrde Street, Brentford
London W13

Peter Purviss
17, Loudwater Place
Kew
London

1 December 20X2

Dear Peter,

Monthly Fees

Thank you for your letter of 24 November.

I note what you say about your cash flow and your difficulty in knowing what level of service charges to set your fellow residents. Indeed, this is a matter of concern to us too especially where we (in theory) hold cash on behalf of our clients. I have already instructed our staff to look into our costing procedures to see if anything can be done and I am hoping that a solution that is not too much of an administrative burden can be arrived at.

With best wishes for Christmas and the New Year

Yours sincerely

Edward

E. Strange

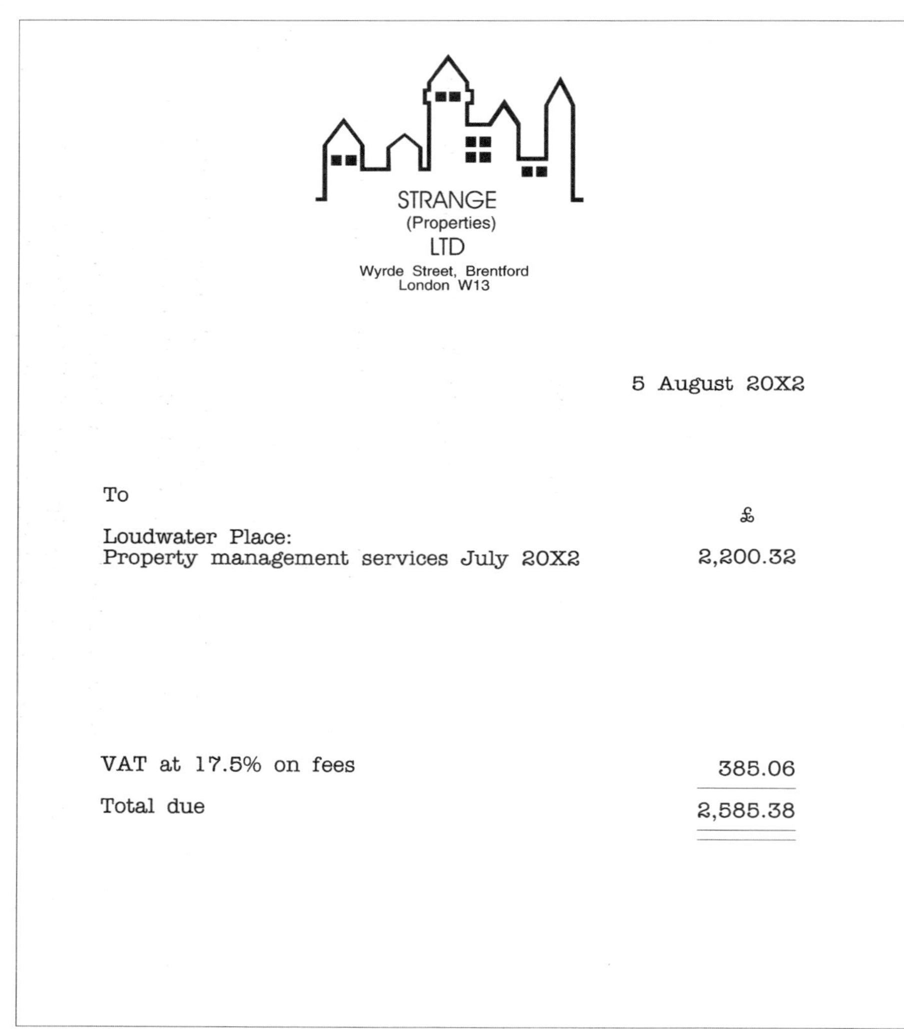

STRANGE
(Properties)
LTD
Wyrde Street, Brentford
London W13

5 August 20X2

To

Loudwater Place:

	£
Property management services July 20X2	2,200.32
VAT at 17.5% on fees	385.06
Total due	2,585.38

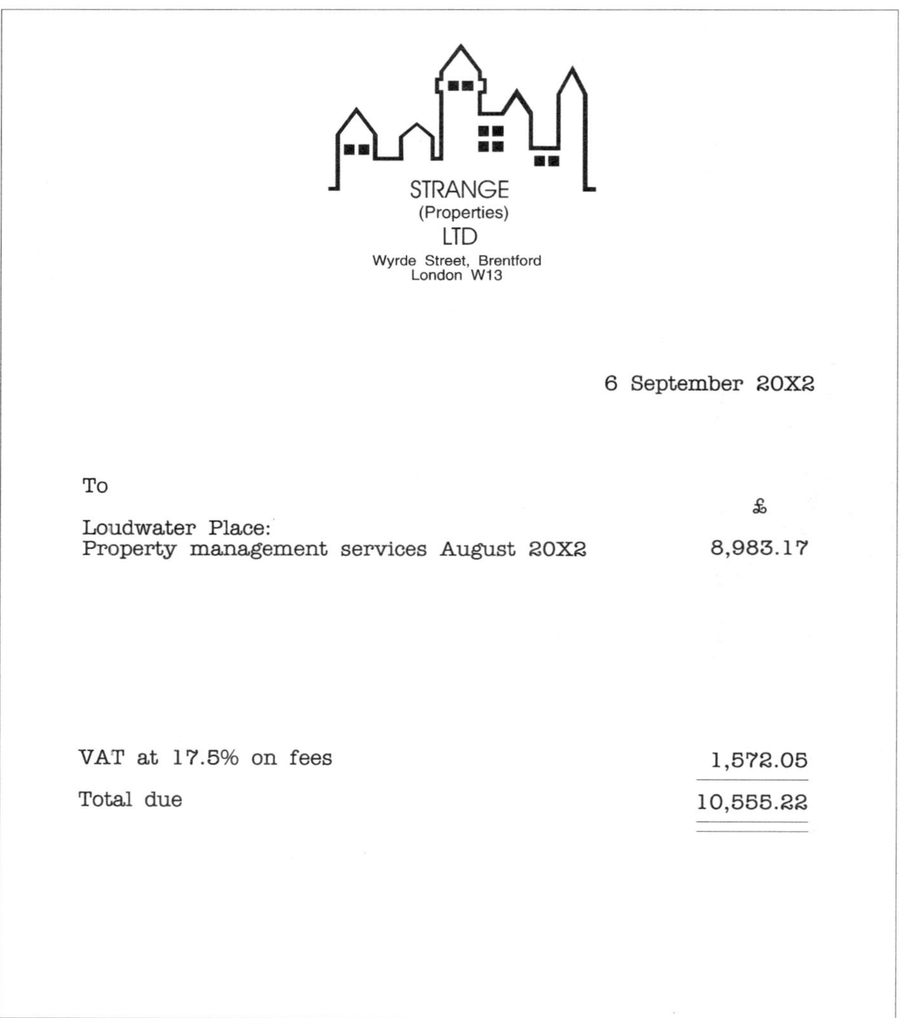

STRANGE
(Properties)
LTD
Wyrde Street, Brentford
London W13

6 September 20X2

To

Loudwater Place:

	£
Property management services August 20X2	8,983.17
VAT at 17.5% on fees	1,572.05
Total due	10,555.22

You are aware that clients' monthly charges are made up as follows.

	£
Direct expenses paid by Strange (Properties) Ltd	X
Fixed fee	1,500.00
One-thirtieth share of overheads incurred in the month	X
	X

The treatment of overheads seems reasonable as far as your own department's services are concerned, because you and your staff do indeed seem to spend a roughly equal amount of time on each client. However you are not sure how fair it is with respect to other work.

In any case you decide to see what the charges for November will be on this basis. You have the cash book for November but this has not yet been coded up for posting. You also have a list of account codes.

Account codes

Range	*Sub-account*	*Name*
100		STAFF COSTS
	/001	Wages
	/002	Salaries
	/003	PAYE and NI
	/010	Staff welfare
	/020	Employer's liability insurance
200		TRAVEL COSTS
	/001	Petrol
	/002	Motor insurance
	/003	Fares and taxis
300		BUILDINGS COSTS
	/001	Heat and light
	/002	Buildings insurance
	/003	Rates
	/004	Repairs and maintenance
	/005	Cleaning
400		COMMUNICATIONS
	/001	Postage
	/002	Telephone
	/003	Stationery
	/004	Computer sundries
500		PROFESSIONAL FEES
	/001	Auditors
	/002	Public liability insurance
	/003	Subscriptions
600		FINANCE CHARGES
	/001	Bank interest
	/002	Bank charges

Range	*Sub-account*	*Name*
700		PUBLICITY
	/001	Advertising
	/002	Entertaining
800		CLIENT CODES
	/001	Rodway House
	/100	Matkins Gardens
	/101	Glebe Gardens
	/105	Gibbs House
	/110	Grasmere Mansion
	/189	Seymour Manor
	/225	Queen's Court
	/250	Loudwater Place
	/261	De Beauvoir Buildings
	/274	Jones Court
	/301	Ashby Mansions
	/325	Kings Buildings
	/350	Clift Flats
	/376	Neville House
	/401	Frampton Court
	/429	Hennigan House
	/430	Wyndham Rise
	/450	Coomer Place
	/501	Laine House
	/525	Undercliff Gardens
	/555	Burgess Court
	/556	Ketley Close
	/605	Mallow Close
	/620	Clifton Gardens
	/675	Endymion Place
	/750	Oakwood Buildings
	/801	Davison Close
	/890	Tilbury Tower
	/914	Rhodes Close
	/999	Clerk Court
900		SUNDRIES
	/001	E S expenses
	/002	V S expenses
	/003	General sundries

No.	Date	Description	Code	Total
	November			£
1	1	Caretaker - Clerk Court		76.50
2	1	Sankey Builders, Sheen - Ketley		600.00
3	1	Post Office		3.61
4	1	Sundries - Gibbs Ho		52.80
5	1	Perivale Glass Co.		317.00
6	3	Motor Mower - Burgess Ct		263.00
7	4	Electricity - Ketley Cl, (to 28,10)		355.84
8	4	Water rates - Q.C		92.00
9	4	Inst, Ch, Surveyors		515.00
10	5	Hanwell DIY		69.10
11	8	Law Society (subs)		742.00
12	8	Inland Revenue		8,437.50
13	8	Gas - Mallow Cl, (to 5.11)		81.50
14	9	Cleaners - Seymour M.		390.01
15	10	Power Drill - Laine Ho.		48.90
16	13	Perivale Roofing		4,720.00
17	17	Dentone (sols) - re Ashby M.		723.37
18	17	Coomer PL - Caretaker		226.00
19	17	Kew Electrics		590.72
20	17	Southern Electricity (to 15.11)		1,110.43
21	17	Wyrde St Computer Supplies		33.00
22	18	Brentford Advertiser		66.50
23	19	Rentokil - Jones Co.		856.06
24	21	Nevill Ho - Skip Hire (17.10-19.11)		32.40
25	21	Hanwell Timber		236.00
26	21	Sankeys - Ketley Clo.		1,800.00
27	24	Heston Service Station		8.81
28	24	Bldgs Ins - Oakwood B		408.00
29	24	Plumbing Supplies (Petersham) Ltd - Kings		426.80
30	24	Wages - Grasmere Caretaker		279.19
31	25	BACS - Salaries		12,187.89
32	25	British Gas - Tilbury		35.60

No.	Date	Description	Code	Total
	November			£
33	26	Hall Hire - Wyndham AGM		32.50
34	26	Sainsbury's		19.50
35	28	Caretaker - Rodway Ho.		438.00
36	28	Property Management News		18.40
37	28	British Telecom		475.70
38	28	Co. House - Wyndham		32.00
39	28	Concrete repairs - Tilbury T		2,250.00
40	28	Acton Skip Hire - 1.11-30.11 - Davison		32.40
41	28	Brentford Cleaning		183.00
42	28	Wages - Davison Clo. C/T		66.10
43	28	Wages - Endymion Pl. C/T		64.50
44	28	Middlesex Gazette		22.22
45	28	Ben Smith Stationery Supplies		178.57
46	28	Electricity - Hennigan Ho. (to 25.11)		568.35
47	28	Guardian Royal Exchange - Pub. Liab		970.00
48	28	Guardian Royal Exchange - Richm.. Bldgs		1,630.00
49	28	E Strange Exps		88.90
50	28	Non-Dom Rates DD		271.25
51	28	GRE Insurance - Jaguar		1,315.50
52	28	Bank - charges		70.90
53	28	Bank - interest		949.93
54				
55				
56				
57				
58				
59				
60				
61				
62				
63				
64				

Tasks

Task 1

(a) Code up the entries in the cash book, allocating the payments either directly to clients or to the appropriate Strange (Properties) Ltd account.

(*Note.* You can assume that geographical references in a cash book entry mean that the cost should be allocated to the buildings in the same location.)

(b) Prepare a schedule of client charges using the current basis for allocating charges. Ignore VAT for the purposes of this part of the exercise.

If any matters occur to you at this stage for your reply to Mr Strange's memo, make rough notes. (You will be writing your reply later.)

Task 2

Amongst the debtors you have been pursuing are five former clients who dispensed with Strange (Properties) Ltd's services earlier in the year. The telephone conversations and letters that you have had have contained comments like 'I don't see why we should subsidise your business!'; 'You do next to nothing for us as far as we know'; 'Why are we paying for building works on your other clients' properties?' and so on.

You decide to see if you can find a way of charging each client a fair proportion of the overheads incurred and to do this you collect or compile the following materials:

(a) A rough plan of the office building

(b) An organisation chart

(c) A copy of Strange (Properties) Ltd's accounts for the year ended 30 September 20X2

(d) A summary of the timesheets of Edward Strange and Victor Strange for the year 20X1/20X2

These documents, or extracts from them, are shown below.

Floor plan

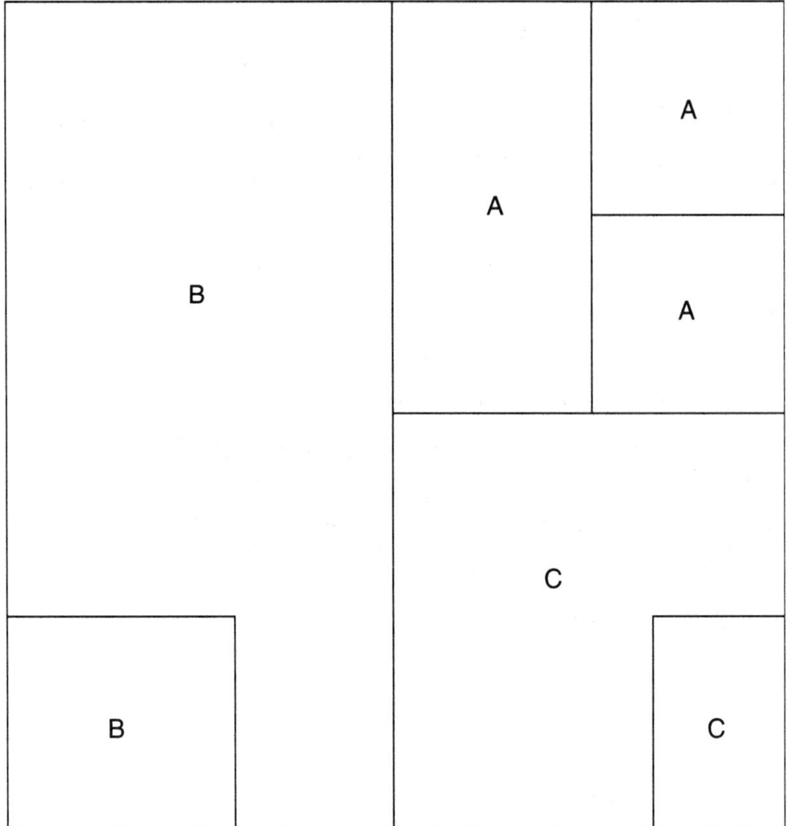

A = Solicitors staff
B = Surveying staff
C = Accounts staff

Organisation chart

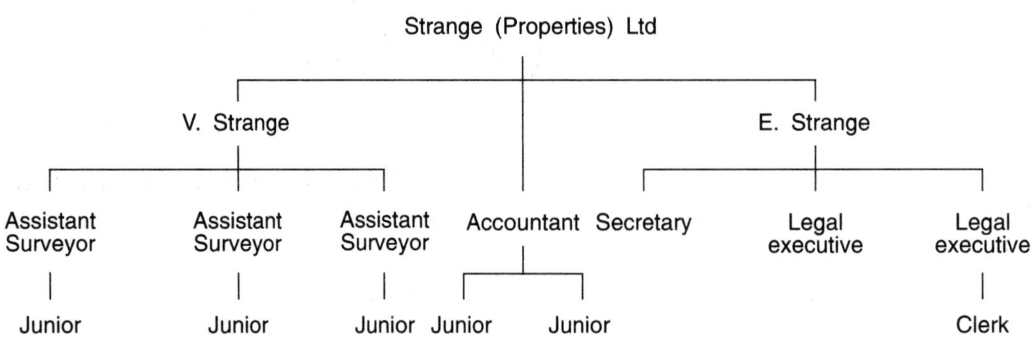

STRANGE (PROPERTIES) LTD
PROFIT AND LOSS ACCOUNT FOR THE YEAR ENDED
30 SEPTEMBER 20X2

	£	£
Fees		1,333,838
Less direct expenses		352,187
		981,651
Less costs of administration		
Wages and salaries	272,255	
Business rates	3,524	
Insurance	7,600	
Heat and light	4,775	
Depreciation of motor vehicles	7,500	
Depreciation of office equipment	1,752	
Repairs and maintenance	834	
Cleaning	6,584	
Depreciation of buildings	4,000	
Staff welfare	1,538	
Telecommunications	1,908	
Printing, postage and stationery	3,975	
Subscriptions	1,131	
Audit and accountancy fees	4,500	
Bank charges	862	
Advertising	1,973	
		324,711
		656,940
Interest payable		10,121
Profit before tax		646,819
Taxation		159,680
Profit for the financial year		487,139
Dividends		475,320
Retained profit transferred to reserves		11,819

STRANGE (PROPERTIES) LTD
BALANCE SHEET AS AT 30 SEPTEMBER 20X2

Fixed assets	*Leased buildings*	*Motor vehicles*	*Office equipment*	*Total*
	£	£	£	£
Cost	80,000	30,000	17,520	127,520
Depreciation	48,000	22,500	7,008	77,508
	32,000	7,500	10,512	50,012
Current assets				
Debtors			309,060	
Prepayments			5,296	
			314,356	
Creditors				
Bank overdraft		113,880		
Other creditors		47,294		
Dividends		50,000		
			211,174	
				103,182
				153,194
Share capital				20,000
Profit and loss account				133,194
				153,194

(*Note.* The motor vehicles are the two second-hand Jaguars used by the Strange brothers. Both cost £15,000.)

TIME SHEET SUMMARY 20X1/X2

	Edward Strange *Hours*	Victor Strange *Hours*
Current clients		
Ashby Mansions	43	20
Burgess Court	71	82
Clerk Court	62	34
Clift Flats	15	113
Clifton Gardens	25	64
Coomer Place	60	80
Davison Close	49	52
De Beauvoir Buildings	74	38
Endymion Place	33	51
Frampton Court	16	73
Gibbs House	51	21
Glebe Gardens	81	60
Grasmere Mansion	84	30
Hennigan House	76	94
Jones Court	61	66
Ketley Close	49	36
Kings Buildings	63	57
Laine House	45	77
Loudwater Place	73	48
Matkins Gardens	76	35
Mallow Close	57	61
Neville House	24	92
Oakwood Buildings	117	40
Queen's Court	51	18
Rhodes Close	82	97
Rodway House	64	88
Seymour Manor	23	64
Tilbury Tower	29	59
Undercliff Gardens	80	71
Wyndham Rise	75	28
Ex-clients		
Anderson Place	14	8
Jacques Court	25	12
Oxford Gardens	22	14
Robin House	20	15
Williams Close	30	22

Your task is to apportion the administrative and publicity expenses and interest shown in the accounts as you think appropriate and to calculate how much should have been charged to each of Strange (Properties) Ltd's current clients.

Task 3

Reply to Mr Strange's memo, offering a solution to his problem. You may, of course, give him a copy of the calculations that you have already done. It would also be helpful to explain to him briefly about different methods of costing, but bear in mind that he has a very limited understanding of accountancy jargon.

2 Practice devolved assessment Stately Hotels plc

Performance criteria

The following performance criteria are covered in this Practice devolved assessment.

Element 6.1: Record and analyse information relating to direct costs

4 Standard costs are compared against actual costs and any variances are analysed

Element 6.2: Record and analyse information relating to the allocation, apportionment and absorption of overhead costs

6 Standard costs are compared against actual costs and any variances are analysed

Element 6.3: Prepare and present standard cost reports

1 Standard cost reports with variances clearly identified are presented in an intelligible form

2 Unusual or unexpected results are identified and reported to managers

3 Any reasons for significant variances from standard are identified and the explanations presented to management

4 The results of the analysis and explanations of specific variances are produced for management

5 Staff working in operational departments are consulted to resolve any queries in the data

Notes on completing the Assessment

This Assessment is designed to test your ability to prepare and present standard cost reports.

You are provided with data on Pages 40 to 42 which you must use to complete the tasks on Pages 41 to 43.

You are allowed **three hours** to complete your work.

A high level of accuracy is required. Check your work carefully.

Correcting fluid should not be used. Errors should be crossed out neatly and clearly. You should write in ink - not pencil.

A FULL SUGGESTED ANSWER TO THIS ASSESSMENT IS PROVIDED ON PAGE 190.

Do not turn to the suggested answer until you have completed all parts of the Assessment.

STATELY HOTELS PLC

Data

SECTION 1

You work as the assistant to the management accountant for a major hotel chain, Stately Hotels plc. The new manager of one of the largest hotels in the chain, The Regent Hotel, is experimenting with the use of standard costing to plan and control the costs of preparing and cleaning the hotel bedrooms.

Two of the costs involved in this activity are cleaning labour and the supply of presentation soap packs.

Cleaning labour

Part-time staff are employed to clean and prepare the bedrooms for customers. The employees are paid for the number of hours that they work, which fluctuates on a daily basis depending on how many rooms need to be prepared each day.

The employees are paid a standard hourly rate for weekday work and a higher hourly rate at the weekend. The standard cost control system is based on an average of these two rates at £7.20 per hour.

The standard time allowed for cleaning and preparing a bedroom is fifteen minutes.

Presentation soap packs

A presentation soap pack is left in each room every night. The packs contain soap, bubble bath, shower gel, hand lotion etc. Most customers use the packs or take them home with them, but many do not. The standard usage of packs used for planning and control purposes is one pack per room per night.

The packs are purchased from a number of different suppliers and the standard price is £1.20 per pack. Stocks of packs are valued in the accounts at standard price.

Actual results for May

During May, 8,400 rooms were cleaned and prepared. The following data was recorded for cleaning labour and soap packs.

Cleaning labour paid for:

Weekday labour	1,850	hours @ £6 per hour
Weekend labour	700	hours @ £9 per hour
	2,550	

Presentation soap packs purchased and used:

6,530	packs @ £1.20 each
920	packs @ £1.30 each
1,130	packs @ £1.40 each
8,580	

Tasks

1 Using the data above, calculate the following cost variances for May:

(a) Soap pack price
(b) Soap pack usage
(c) Cleaning labour rate
(d) Cleaning labour utilisation or efficiency

2 Suggest one possible cause for each of the variances which you have calculated.

SECTION 2

Data

You are employed as the assistant management accountant to Albion Ltd. Albion Ltd manufactures a single product, the Xtra, an ingredient used in food processing. The basic raw material in Xtra production is material X. The average unit prices for material X in each quarter last year are reproduced below.

	Quarter 1	*Quarter 2*	*Quarter 3*	*Quarter 4*
Average unit price of X	£10	£11	£16	£19

Albion Ltd operates a standard absorption costing system. Standards are established at the beginning of each year. Each week the management accounting section prepares a statement for the production director reconciling the actual cost of production with its standard cost. Standard costing data for week 8 of quarter 4 in the current year is given below.

Standard costing and budget data for week 8 of quarter 4, 20X0			
	Quantity	*Unit price*	*Cost per unit*
Material (kilograms)	3	£23.00	£69
Labour (hours)	2	£20.00	£40
Fixed overheads (hours)	2	£60.00	£120
Standard unit cost			£229
Budgeted production for week 8	*Budgeted units*	*Standard cost per unit*	*Standard cost of production*
	10,000	£229	£2,290,000

During week 8, production of Xtra totalled 9,000 units and the actual costs for that week were:

Inputs	*Units*	*Total cost*
Materials (kilograms)	26,500	£662,500
Labour (hours)	18,400	£349,600
Fixed overheads (hours)	18,400	£1,500,000

Using this data, a colleague has already calculated the fixed overhead variances. These were as follows:

- Fixed overhead expenditure variance £300,000 adverse
- Fixed overhead efficiency (or usage) variance £24,000 adverse
- Fixed overhead capacity variance £96,000 adverse

Tasks

Your colleague asks you to:

1 Calculate the following variances:

(a) material price
(b) material usage
(c) labour rate
(d) labour efficiency

2 Prepare a statement listing all of the cost variances.

SECTION 3

Data

You are employed as an accounting technician in a large industrial company which operates a four-weekly system of management reporting. Your division, division X, makes a single product, the Alpha. The nature of the production process means that there is no work in progress at any time.

The group accountant has completed the calculation of the material and labour standard costing variances for the current period to 1 December but has not had the time to calculate any other variances. Details of the variances already calculated are produced in the working papers below, along with other standard costing data.

Standard costing and budget data - four weeks ended 1 December 20X0			
	Quantity	*Unit price*	*Cost per unit*
Material (litres)	40	£4.00	£160
Labour (hours)	10	£8.40	£84
Fixed overheads (hours)	10	£6.70	£67
Standard cost per unit			£311
	Units	*Standard unit cost*	*Standard cost of production*
Budgeted production	12,000	£311	£3,732,000

Working papers:

Actual production and expenditure for the four weeks ended 1 December 20X0

Units produced	11,200
Cost of 470,000 litres of material consumed	£1,974,000
Cost of 110,000 labour hours worked	£935,000
Expenditure on fixed overheads	£824,000

Material and labour variances

Material price variance	£94,000	(A)
Material usage variance	£88,000	(A)
Labour rate variance	£11,000	(A)
Labour efficiency variance	£16,800	(F)

Tasks

1 Calculate the following variances.

(a) The fixed overhead expenditure variance
(b) The fixed overhead volume variance
(c) The fixed overhead capacity variance
(d) The fixed overhead efficiency variance

2 Prepare a report for presentation to the production director showing the cost variances for the four weeks ended 1 December 20X0.

3 The production director, who has only recently been appointed, is unfamiliar with fixed overhead variances. Because of this, the group management accountant has asked you to prepare a *brief* memo to the production director.

Your memo should do the following.

(a) Explain what is meant by the fixed overhead expenditure, volume, capacity and efficiency variances.

(b) Suggest one possible cause for each of the variances that you have calculated.

Trial run devolved assessment

TRIAL RUN DEVOLVED ASSESSMENT

FOOD WITH A BITE

INTERMEDIATE STAGE - NVQ/SVQ3

Unit 6

Recording Cost Information

The purpose of this Trial Run Devolved Assessment is to give you an idea of what an AAT Simulation looks like. It is not intended as a definitive guide to the tasks you may be required to perform.

The suggested time allowance for this Assessment is **four hours**.

Calculators may be used but no reference material is permitted.

DO NOT OPEN THIS PAPER UNTIL YOU ARE READY TO START UNDER TIMED CONDITIONS

INSTRUCTIONS

This Assessment is designed to test your ability to record cost information.

Background information is provided on Page 49.

The tasks you are to perform are set out on Pages 50 and 51.

You are provided with data on Pages 51 to 64 which you must use to complete the tasks.

Your answers should be set out in the answer booklet on Pages 67 to 72 using the documents provided. You may require additional answer pages.

You are allowed **four hours** to complete your work.

A high level of accuracy is required. Check your work carefully.

Correcting fluid may not be used. Errors should be crossed out neatly and clearly. You should write in black ink, not pencil.

You are advised to read the whole of the Assessment before commencing as all of the information may be of value and is not necessarily supplied in the sequence in which you might wish to deal with it.

A FULL SUGGESTED ANSWER TO THIS ASSESSMENT IS PROVIDED ON PAGE 197.

THE SITUATION

It is your first day at your new job. You should have started as the accountant at Food with a Bite Ltd four weeks ago (1 March 20X3), the company's first day of business. A broken leg from a rather nasty fall on the Matterhorn during a skiing holiday has, however, delayed your joining the company.

You arrive on Monday 29 March knowing that you have four weeks work to catch up on but nobody seems to be around the factory or offices apart from Fred and Ali, the two production line workers. They explain that their supervisor is dealing with a delivery, the storekeeper won't be starting for another week (his wife has had a baby and so Harry Jordan, the General Manager, has given him five weeks paternity leave) and that Harry Jordan himself is out of the office for the day. However they point you in the direction of your desk, where all that you need has been left.

On your desk you find three piles of documents marked financial accounts, management accounts and cost accounts and a note from Harry Jordan.

It seems as if you are going to have to cope on your own for the day and you quickly try to assemble in your mind all that you know about Food with a Bite Ltd from your conversations with Harry Jordan at your interviews.

(a) The company began trading on 1 March 20X3.

(b) It makes two products, a hot vegetarian chilli in the chilli production department and a spicy vegetarian curry in the curry production department.

(c) Two production line workers are employed. Ali is initially working on the chilli production line and Fred is initially working on the curry production line. Eventually they will both work on either production line as demand dictates. They are overseen by a supervisor. A storekeeper (when he finally begins working) will look after the stores area (the company's other department). He will spend half of his time controlling the chilli ingredients and half of his time controlling the curry ingredients.

(d) The company's year is divided into 13 four-week periods.

(e) There is a great demand for the two products. Sam's Supermarkets have agreed to take (on a Friday) whatever has been produced during the week.

You pick up Harry's note.

Friday 26 March

Sorry to leave you in the lurch! Hope I've left everything you're going to need on your desk.
Can you start with cost accounting because I desperately need your help for the board meeting on Friday. I've got to take standard cost cards for our two products with me and give them some idea about how efficiently Fred has been working over the last four weeks. The board also want to know how efficiently he's been using the vegetables in the curry.
Do you think you can prepare the cards (I don't know what they are but the board gave me a couple of blanks) and find out about Fred and the vegetables? The board also expect to see updated stores ledger accounts (whatever they are) for lentils and vegetables. Again, they've given me a couple of blanks.
Thanks very much. See you on Wednesday.

Harry

TASKS TO BE COMPLETED

In the answer booklet on Pages 67 to 72 complete the tasks outlined below. Data for this assessment is provided on Pages 51 to 64.

As you complete each of the tasks you should note any matters which need discussing with members of staff, on a schedule of queries, indicating who you will need to speak to and any action which may be necessary. You should ignore VAT and employer's National Insurance contributions and work to two decimal places.

(a) Calculate standard material costs for a vegetarian chilli and a vegetarian curry, basing the standard quantities on the information provided by Delia Craddock and the standard prices on the expected prices at 1 September 20X3. (Materials includes cartons.)

Fill in the details of the standard quantities and standard prices, and hence the standard material costs, on each of the standard cost cards.

(b) Calculate standard labour costs for a vegetarian chilli and a vegetarian curry using information from the business plan and the offers of employment.

Fill in the details of the standard times and standard wage rates, and hence the standard labour costs, on each of the standard cost cards.

(c) Calculate standard variable overhead costs for a vegetarian chilli and a vegetarian curry using information provided by Oly from Oly's Oils.

Fill in the details of the standard quantity and standard price, and hence the standard overhead cost, on each of the standard cost cards.

(d) (i) Calculate the budgeted annual fixed overheads, fixed overheads being the salaries of the supervisor and storekeeper, the cost of cleaners, heat and light and overtime premium.

(ii) Allocate overheads direct to departments where possible.

(iii) Apportion the remaining overheads between the three departments using suitable bases (budgeted direct labour hours, floor area and overtime hours).

(iv) Apportion the service department overheads to the two production departments.

(v) Calculate departmental overhead absorption rates based on direct labour hours.

Fill in the details of the standard fixed overhead absorbed into each product on the standard cost card. You should now have two completed standard cost cards.

(e) Calculate a labour efficiency variance for the curry department for the four-week period using details from the clock cards and standard cost card and the fact that 5,000 portions of curry were made.

(f) Complete (as fully as possible, given the available information) a stores record card for the four-week period for lentils and for vegetables using the information provided in the list of what was taken from the storeroom and the two Exotic Foods Emporium invoices. Use the stock valuation method recommended in the business plan.

(g) Calculate a usage variance for the vegetables used during the four-week period using information on the appropriate stores record card and standard cost card. You are reminded that 5,000 portions of curry were made.

(h) Calculate any under or over absorption of fixed overhead during the four-week period. You are informed that 5,300 portions of chilli were made. To determine the cost of overtime premium incurred you need to know, in addition to the information you already have, that Ali worked a total of 7.25 hours overtime.

DATA

(a) The following letter and list of ingredients were received from Delia Craddock.

Mr H. Jordan
Food With a Bite Ltd
Spicy Court
Riceford

Apple Cottage
Rose Lane
Little Smedlingford

23rd February 20X3

Dear Harry

What a lovely surprise hearing from you after so many years. Yes, of course I remember our days at University together. How could I forget!! Do you remember that poem you recited to me as we punted down the river?

I'm so pleased your business empire is expanding and I'd love to help in any way I can. I enclose a list of the standard ingredients for vegetarian chilli and vegetarian curry. I hope it's what you needed.

I look forward to seeing you on the 29 March. I'll be in black!

Enclosed

Delia

Delia Craddock

Standard ingredients for one portion

Vegetarian chilli

0.125 kg rice
0.0625 kg lentils
0.167 kg tinned tomatoes
0.167 kg mushroom/onion/pepper mixture
0.167 kg kidney beans
0.025 kg dried chillies

Vegetarian curry

0.125 kg rice
0.167 litres coconut oil
0.005 kg spices
0.167 kg vegetables

(b) The following compliments slip and current price list were received from Exotic Foods Emporium.

Please find enclosed current price list. As to your enquiry, our prices have increased by 10% since 1.3.X2. It is likely that our prices will increase by a similar percentage during the coming year.

With Compliments

Exotic Foods Emporium
The Industrial Estate
Riceford
0321 909 698

PRICE LIST at 1.3.X3

	£
Chillis - 50 kg drum	86.50
Coconut oil - 100 l drum	115.00
Kidney beans - 50 kg drum	44.00
Lentils - 100 kg sack	84.00
Mushroom/onion/pepper - 50 kg drum	58.00
Rice - 100 kg sack	130.00
Spices - 10 kg drum	92.00
Tomatoes - 50 kg drum	35.00
Vegetables - 50 kg drum	53.50

(c) The following quotation was received from a carton manufacturer.

The Container Company   Matfield Road   Riceford

QUOTATION

25/2/X3

Plastic food containers (1 portion) with appropriate design on cardboard lid: unit price 4p.

Price increase to 5p from 1.4.X3. Fixed for 12 months.

(d) The following extract from the Business Plan for Food with a Bite Ltd was prepared by Smethick & Co (Management Consultants).

Extracts from Business Plan

for

Food with a Bite Ltd

by

Smethick & Co
(Management Consultants)

Expected production for 12 months (13 periods) to 28.2.X4

Vegetarian chilli - 78,000 portions
Vegetarian curry - 66,300 portions

Expected labour time to produce 1 portion

Vegetarian chilli - 1.5 minutes
Vegetarian curry - 2 minutes

Per discussion with National Electricity

Likely charge per annum for heat and light £5,000

Recommendations

Initially, value issues and stock using weighted average method. Standard costing will be used once the company and its operations are established.

Absorb overheads on basis of direct labour hours.

Do not allow annual overtime to exceed 100 hours in total for both production line workers. Overtime should not be regular occurrence once system established.

(e) The following offers of employment were sent out in the middle of February.

Food with a Bite
Spicy Court
Riceford

Mr A Khan
132 The Drive
Riceford

20 February 20X3

Dear Mr Khan

I have great pleasure in offering you the position of production line worker (chilli) at Food with a Bite.

Your basic rate of pay will be £4.00 per hour. Any hours worked over and above the basic time of eight hours a day will be paid at time and a half. During your first year of service you are entitled to one week's holiday. This will be increased to four weeks in your second year of service.

I look forward to hearing from you in the very near future.

Yours sincerely

Harry Jordan

Harry Jordan

Food with a Bite

Spicy Court
Riceford

Mr F Jarvis
44 The Close
Riceford

20 February 20X3

Dear Mr Jarvis

I have great pleasure in offering you the position of production line worker (curry) at Food with a Bite.

Your basic rate of pay will be £4.00 per hour. Any hours worked over and above the basic time of eight hours a day will be paid at time and a half. During your first year of employment you are entitled to one week's holiday. This will be increased to four weeks in your second year of service.

I look forward to hearing from you in the very near future.

Yours sincerely

Harry Jordan

Harry Jordan

Food with a Bite

Spicy Court
Riceford

Mr J Simpson
4 The Street
Riceford

20 February 20X3

Dear Mr Simpson

I have great pleasure in offering you the position of production line supervisor at Food with a Bite.

Your starting salary will be £16,000 per annum with an annual review on 1 April 20X4 and every April thereafter. You are entitled to four weeks' holiday per annum.

I look forward to hearing from you in the very near future.

Yours sincerely

Harry Jordan

Harry Jordan

Food with a Bite

Spicy Court
Riceford

Mr K Sampson
2 The Road
Riceford

20 February 20X3

Dear Mr Sampson

I have great pleasure in offering you the position of Storekeeper at Food with a Bite.

Your starting salary will be £12,000 per annum with an annual review on 1 April 20X4 and every April thereafter. You are entitled to four weeks' holiday per annum.

I look forward to hearing from you in the very near future.

Yours sincerely

Harry Jordan

Harry Jordan

(f) The following telephone message was taken on the 15th March 20X3.

> **Telephone Message**
>
> Mr Jordan
>
> **while you were out**
>
> Oly from Oly's Oils **called**
>
> **at** 9.00 **on** 15/3/X3
>
> **Message** Will supply lubricating oil for the two production line machines @ £17.50 per 10 litre drum. Said to tell you price hasn't changed for last 4 years and unlikely to in future. You'll probably need to use 1 litre of oil per machine for every 100 portions produced by machine.

(g) The following contract is for cleaning the factory and stores of Food with a Bite Ltd.

> Mrs Mopp Cleaners
>
> **Contract**
>
> With: Food with a Bite Ltd
Spicy Court
Riceford
>
> From: 1/3/X3
>
> To: 28/2/X4
>
> For: 2 hours cleaning per night
(factory and stores areas)
>
> At: £10 per hour
>
> For Mrs Mopp Cleaners: V. Rix (Director)
>
> For: Food with a Bite Ltd N. Richards (Director)

(h) The following floor plan shows the factory and stores area.

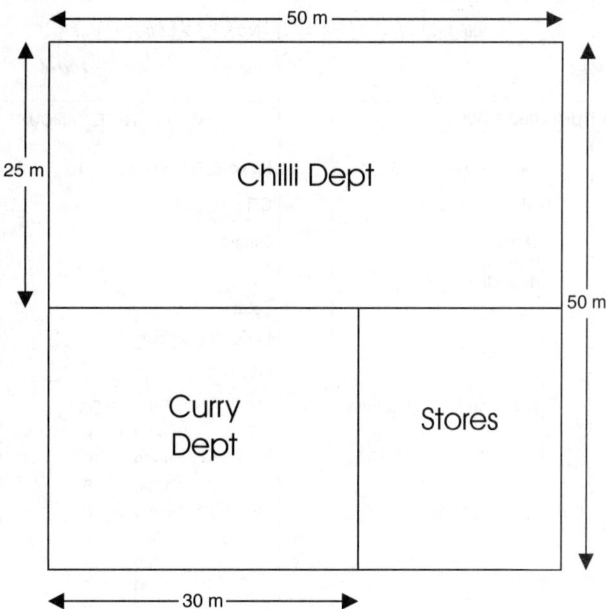

(i) The following electricity bill was received at the end of March 20X3.

NATIONAL ELECTRICITY

YOUR CUSTOMER SERVICES OFFICE IS:	YOU CAN PHONE US ON:
POWER ROAD RICEFORD	0321 949 494

FOOD WITH A BITE LTD
SPICY COURT
RICEFORD

WHEN TELEPHONING
We have a call queuing system. When you hear the ringing tone please wait for a reply as calls are answered in strict rotation.
BUSY TIMES
Please try to avoid 9-30AM - 10-30 AM and 2 PM to 3 PM

METER READING PRESENT	METER READING PREVIOUS	UNITS USED	UNIT PRICE (pence)	V.A.T code	AMOUNT £
2359 E	-	2359	17.470	1	412.12
STANDING CHARGE				1	217.50
TOTAL CHARGE (EXCLUDING VAT)					629.62
VAT 1 629.62 @ 17.5% COMMERCIAL					110.18

MAKE YOUR BILLS EASIER TO SWALLOW - SEE PAGE 4 OF 'SOURCE' FOR BUDGET SCHEME APPLICATION

E=Estimated reading. Please read carefully the advice given on the back of this bill
C=Your own reading

BALANCE TO PAY			739.80
VAT CHARGE THIS BILL			110.18
YOUR ACCOUNT NUMBER	BILL DATE/TAX POINT	READING DATE	NON-DOMESTIC USE
34721193672	26.03.X3	26.03.X3	100%

(j) The following four clock cards cover the four weeks ending 26 March 20X3.

No 101 Ending 5/3/X3

Name Fred Jarvis

	HOURS	RATE	AMOUNT	DEDUCTIONS	
Basic				Income Tax	
O/T				NI	
Others				Other	
				Total deduction	
Total					
Less deductions					
Net due					

Time	Day	Basic time	Overtime
1630	F		
1330	F		
1230	F		
0800	F		
1700	T		
1330	T		
1230	T		
0830	T		
1830	W		
1330	W		
1300	W		
0800	W		
1700	T		
1330	T		
1230	T		
0830	T		
1700	M		
1330	M		
1230	M		
0830	M		

Signature

No 101 Ending 12/3/X3

Name Fred Jarvis

	HOURS	RATE	AMOUNT	DEDUCTIONS	
Basic				Income Tax	
O/T				NI	
Others				Other	
				Total deduction	
Total					
Less deductions					
Net due					

Time	Day	Basic time	Overtime
1630	F		
1330	F		
1200	F		
0800	F		
1800	T		
1330	T		
1230	T		
0800	T		
1630	W		
1330	W		
1230	W		
0730	W		
1630	T		
1330	T		
1230	T		
0730	T		
1630	M		
1330	M		
1230	M		
0730	M		

Signature

No 101 Ending 19/3/X3
Name Fred Jarvis

	HOURS	RATE	AMOUNT	DEDUCTIONS	
Basic				Income Tax	
O/T				NI	
Others				Other	
				Total deduction	
Total					
Less deductions					
Net due					

Time	Day	Basic time	Overtime
1700	F		
1330	F		
1230	F		
0830	F		
1730	T		
1330	T		
1300	T		
0800	T		
1730	W		
1330	W		
1300	W		
0730	W		
1800	T		
1400	T		
1330	T		
0700	T		
1700	M		
1330	M		
1230	M		
0830	M		

Signature ....

No 101 Ending 26/3/X3
Name Fred Jarvis

	HOURS	RATE	AMOUNT	DEDUCTIONS	
Basic				Income Tax	
O/T				NI	
Others				Other	
				Total deduction	
Total					
Less deductions					
Net due					

Time	Day	Basic time	Overtime
1800	F		
1400	F		
1330	F		
0730	F		
1830	T		
1430	T		
1400	T		
0800	T		
1730	W		
1330	W		
1230	W		
0830	W		
1730	T		
1330	T		
1300	T		
0800	T		
1800	M		
1330	M		
1230	M		
0730	M		

Signature ....

(k) The following list shows what Fred and Ali took from stores.

What we took from storeroom

Mon 1 March
- 1 sack/drum of each food stuff
- 2,000 cartons

Wed 3 March
- 2 rice
- 3 toms
- 3 mush
- 3 kidney
- 2,000 cartons
- 1 coconut
- 3 veg

Mon 8 March
- 5 veg
- 5 rice
- 1 lentil
- 5 toms
- 5 mush
- 5 kidney
- 3,000 cartons
- 2 coconut
- 1 spice

Mon 15 March
- 2 rice
- 1 lentil
- 4 toms
- 4 mush
- 4 kidneys
- 2,000 cartons
- 2 coconut
- 1 spice
- 4 veg
- 1 chilli

Mon 22 March
- 3 rice
- 1 lentil
- 1 chilli
- 5 toms
- 5 kidney
- 5 mush
- 3,000 cartons
- 3 coconut
- 5 veg

Fri 26 March
no stock left in production line area

Whenever we took rice or cartons, I had half for chilli and Fred took half for curry

(1) The following two invoices were received from Exotic Foods Emporium.

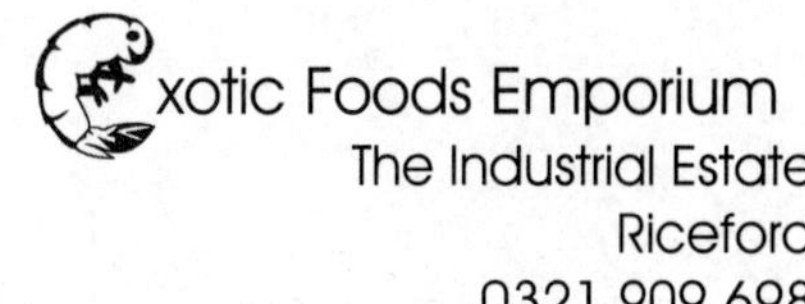

The Industrial Estate
Riceford
0321 909 698

Food with a Bite Ltd
Spicy Court
Riceford

INVOICE

Order no: 0001 Del date: 1/3/X3 Invoice no: 7164 Date: 1/3/X3

Quantity	Description	Unit price £	Total £
10	Rice - 100 kg sack	130.00	1,300.00
4	Lentils - 100 kg sack	84.00	336.00
10	Tomatoes - 50 kg drum	35.00	350.00
10	Mushs etc - 50 kg drum	58.00	580.00
10	Vegetables - 50 kg drum	53.50	535.00
6	Coconut oil - 100 l drum	115.00	690.00
3	Spice - 10 kg tin	92.00	276.00
10	Kidney beans - 50 kg drum	44.00	440.00
2	Chillis - 50 kg drum	86.50	173.00
		Total	**4,680.00**

This agrees with what was delivered
Fred Jarvis
1/3/X3

The Industrial Estate
Riceford
0321 909 698

Food with a Bite Ltd
Spicy Court
Riceford

INVOICE

Order no: 0003 Del date: 12/3/X3 Invoice no: 7321 Date: 12/3/X3

Quantity	Description	Unit price £	Total £
4	Rice - 100 kg sack	131.00	524.00
10	Tomatoes - 50 kg drum	35.00	350.00
10	Mushs etc - 50 kg drum	58.50	585.00
11	Vegetables - 50 kg drum	53.75	591.25
4	Coconut oil - 100 l drum	118.00	472.00
12	Kidney beans - 50 kg drum	44.00	528.00
3	Chillis - 50 kg drum	86.50	259.50
		Total	3,309.75

Only 2 drums of chillis delivered
but 5 sacks of rice came
Fred Jarvis
12/3/X3

TRIAL RUN DEVOLVED ASSESSMENT

FOOD WITH A BITE

ANSWER BOOKLET

Documents for use in this Assessment

The documents you will need to prepare the solution are given on Pages 67 to 72 and consist of two blank standard cost cards and two blank stores record cards. Pages 70 to 72 are blank and can be used for any written solutions, calculations or workings.

Standard cost cards

STANDARD COST CARD

PRODUCT Veg chilli

DESCRIPTION	QUANTITY	COST PER KG/HOUR/ETC	EXTENSION	TOTAL
Materials		£	£	£
Rice	0·125kg	1·37	0·17	
lentils	0·0625kg	0·88	0·06	
Tin Tomatoes	0·167kg	0·74	0·12	
Mushroom/onion Pepper	0·167kg	1·22	0·20	
Kidney beans	0·167kg	0·92	0·15	
Dried chillies	0·025kg	1·82	0·05	
Carton	1	0·05	0·05	
SUB-TOTAL				0·80
Labour				
SUB-TOTAL				
Direct cost				
Variable o/h				
Standard variable cost				
Fixed o/h				
Standard cost of sale				

STANDARD COST CARD

PRODUCT ....

DESCRIPTION	QUANTITY	COST PER KG/HOUR/ETC	EXTENSION	TOTAL
Materials		£	£	£
SUB-TOTAL				
Labour				
SUB-TOTAL				
Direct cost				
Variable o/h				
Standard variable cost				
Fixed o/h				
Standard cost of sale				

Stores record cards

STORES RECORD CARD

Material: .... Maximum Quantity: ....

Code: .... Minimum Quantity: ....

Date	Receipts				Issues				Stock		
	G.R.N. No.	Quantity	Unit Price £	Amount £	Material Req. No.	Quantity	Unit Price £	Amount £	Quantity	Unit Price £	Amount £

STORES RECORD CARD

Material: .... Maximum Quantity: ....

Code: .... Minimum Quantity: ....

Date	Receipts				Issues				Stock		
	G.R.N. No.	Quantity	Unit Price £	Amount £	Material Req. No.	Quantity	Unit Price £	Amount £	Quantity	Unit Price £	Amount £

Blank 1

Blank 2

Blank 3

AAT SAMPLE SIMULATION

INTERMEDIATE STAGE - NVQ/SVQ3

Unit 6

Recording Cost Information

This Sample Simulation is the AAT's Sample Simulation for Unit 6. Its purpose is to give you an idea of what an AAT simulation looks like. It is not intended as a definitive guide to the tasks you may be required to perform.

The suggested time allowance for this Assessment is four hours. Up to 30 minutes extra time may be permitted in an AAT simulation. Breaks in assessment may be allowed in the AAT simulation, but it must normally be completed in one day.

Calculators may be used but no reference material is permitted.

DO NOT OPEN THIS PAPER UNTIL YOU ARE READY TO START UNDER TIMED CONDITIONS

INSTRUCTIONS

This Simulation is designed to test your ability to record cost information.

Background information is provided on Page 75.

The tasks you are to perform are set out on Pages 76 to 77.

You are provided with data on Pages 78 to 87 which you must use to complete the tasks.

Your answers should be set out in the answer booklet on Pages 91 to 102 using the documents provided. You may require additional answer pages.

You are allowed **four hours** to complete your work.

A high level of accuracy is required. Check your work carefully.

Correcting fluid may not be used. Errors should be crossed out neatly and clearly. You should write in black ink, not pencil.

You are advised to read the whole of the Simulation before commencing as all of the information may be of value and is not necessarily supplied in the sequence in which you might wish to deal with it.

A FULL SUGGESTED ANSWER TO THIS SIMULATION IS PROVIDED IN THIS KIT ON PAGES 205.

THE SITUATION

Introduction

Your name is Lesley Hunt and you work as an accounts assistant for Polycot Ltd, a manufacturer of cotton duvet covers.

Cost centres

The production cost centres in Polycot Ltd are a cutting department, a finishing department and a packing department.

- Work in the cutting department is machine-intensive. The machines are operated by a number of direct employees.
- Work in the finishing department and packing department is labour-intensive, and is carried out entirely by direct employees of Polycot Ltd.

In addition to the production cost centres there is also a stores department.

Cost accounting records

Polycot Ltd uses the FIFO method for valuing issues of materials to production and stocks of materials.

The company is registered for VAT and all of its outputs are standard-rated. This means that VAT on its purchases can always be reclaimed and should therefore be ignored in the cost records.

The accounts code list for the company includes the following codes:

Cost centre codes		*Expenditure codes*	
C100	Cutting department	E200	Direct materials
C200	Finishing department	E210	Indirect materials
C300	Packing department	E300	Direct wages
C400	Stores	E310	Indirect wages
		E410	Indirect revenue expenses
		E500	Depreciation - production equipment

Until now, the company has absorbed all production overheads on the basis of a percentage of direct labour costs. However, as you will see, a change is proposed in this area for the coming year. Whatever method of overhead absorption is used, any under or over absorption is transferred to the profit and loss account at the end of each quarter.

Personnel

The personnel involved in the simulation are as follows:

Production manager	Jim Stubbs
General manager	Patrick McGrath

In the simulation you will begin by dealing with certain transactions in the month of March 1998, and you will then be involved in forecasting outcomes for the company's financial year ending 31 March 1999. Finally, you will use your results to account for transactions in July 1998. Note that for many of the tasks you will need to prepare rough workings; you should use the paper provided for this purpose on Page 103 of the answer booklet.

TASKS TO BE COMPLETED

Part 1: Transactions in March 1998

1 Refer to the invoices and materials requisitions on Pages 78 - 82. Using this information you are required to complete the stores ledger accounts on Pages 91 and 92 of the answer booklet for the month of March 1998. You are reminded that the company uses the FIFO method. You may assume that suppliers raise invoices on the same day as goods are delivered.

2 You are required to prepare a memo for the general manager, Patrick McGrath, drawing attention to any unusual matters concerning stock levels of the items dealt with in task 1 above. Use the blank memo form on Page 93 of the answer booklet and date your memo 3 April 1998.

3 Timesheets for two employees of Polycot Ltd are shown on Pages 94 and 95 of the answer booklet. These employees work on production of duvet covers. Using the information contained in the internal policy document on Page 83 of this booklet, you are required to analyse their wages for the week ending 6 March 1998, as follows:

- Complete the total column in each timesheet.
- Check for discrepancies and make any necessary adjustments.
- Calculate the bonus earned by each employee on each day and in total for the week, and enter the appropriate amounts on the timesheets.
- Complete the analysis at the bottom of each timesheet.
- Enter the appropriate figures on the cost ledger data entry sheet on Page 96 of the answer booklet.

4 Prepare a memo to the production manager, Jim Stubbs, outlining any discrepancies in the wages data for these two employees for the week and requesting assistance in resolving your queries. Use the blank memo form on Page 97 of the answer booklet and date your memo 10 March 1998.

Part 2: Overhead absorption for 1998/99

5 The company at present absorbs all production overheads as a percentage of direct labour costs. The company is considering a revision in this policy for the accounting year 1998/99. Under the proposed new policy, a machine hour rate would be used in the cutting department, and direct labour hour rates in the finishing and packing departments. You are required to write a memo to the production manager, Jim Stubbs, explaining why this proposal is appropriate. Use the blank memo form on Page 98 of the answer booklet and date your memo 10 March 1998.

6 Refer to the information given on Page 84. Using this information, you are required to calculate 1998/99 overhead absorption rates for each production department: cutting (machine hour rate), finishing (direct labour hour rate) and packing (direct labour hour rate). Use the analysis sheet on Page 99 of the answer booklet.

7 Refer to the memo on Page 85. You are required to use the information in this memo to perform the following tasks:

(a) Write a memo to the production manager, Jim Stubbs, concerning the query on the wages for the temporary employee. Explain precisely and clearly what information you would need to be able to fully analyse and classify the hours worked by the employee and the wages paid. Use the blank memo form on Page 100 of the answer booklet and date your memo 6 July 1998.

For the remainder of this task, you are required to ignore the pending query concerning the temporary employee.

(b) Using the overhead absorption rate that you calculated in task 6 and the information contained in the labour hours analysis, calculate the production overhead absorbed in the packing department during the quarter ending 30 June 1998. Insert your result in the working sheet on Page 100 of the answer booklet.

(c) Using the information on the costs charged to cost centre code C300, determine the total actual production overhead cost for the packing department for the quarter ending 30 June 1998. Insert your result in the working sheet on Page 100 of the answer booklet.

(d) Determine the amount to be transferred to the profit and loss account for the quarter ending 30 June 1998, in respect of under or over absorbed production overheads for the packing department. Indicate clearly whether the overheads are under or over absorbed for the quarter.

Part 3: Standard costs and variances, July 1998

8 Refer to the information on Page 86. Using this information you are required to complete the standard cost card on Page 101 of the answer booklet. Note that you may need to refer to the following information: your completed stores ledger accounts on Pages 91 and 92 of the answer booklet; the direct labour hour rates on Page 83; and the overhead absorption rates that you calculated in task 6.

9 Refer to the memo on Page 87. You are required to prepare a memo, addressed to the general manager, Patrick McGrath, analysing all of the variances arising during the week ended 8 July 1998 in the cutting department and suggesting possible reasons for the main variances. You should date your memo 13 July 1998. Use the memo form on Page 102 of the answer booklet.

Note. In addition to the information referred to above, you will also need to refer to the overhead absorption rates that you calculated in task 6 and the standard cost card that you prepared in task 8.

SALES INVOICE

Kenilworth Limited
12 Luton Road, Mapleton, Bedfordshire LU4 8EN
Telephone: 01582 622411

VAT registration: 291 8753 42

Date/tax point: 2 March 1998

Invoice to:
Polycot Limited
17 Hightown Road
Branston BN4 3EW

Invoice number: 2078

Your order: 3901

Item description	**Quantity**	**Unit price £**	**Trade discount @ 30% £**	**Net price £**	**Total £**
Plastic poppers (100 in each box)	100 boxes	91.00	27.30	63.70	6,370.00
Total					6,370.00
VAT @ 17.5%					1,114.75
Total due					7,484.75
Terms: net 30 days					

SALES INVOICE

Baxter Limited
39 Langdale Avenue, Bisham MW3 9TY
Telephone: 01693 77612

VAT registration: 215 8761 34

Date/tax point: 6 March 1998

Invoice to:
Polycot Limited
17 Hightown Road
Branston BN4 3EW

Invoice number: 7123

Your order: 3889

Item description	**Quantity**	**Unit price £**	**Trade discount @ 30% £**	**Net price £**	**Total £**
Cotton - 50 metre rolls	90	124.00	37.20	86.80	7,812.00
Total					7,812.00
VAT @ 17.5%					1,367.10
Total due					9,179.10
Terms: net 30 days					

SALES INVOICE

Kenilworth Limited
12 Luton Road, Mapleton, Bedfordshire LU4 8EN
Telephone: 01582 622411

VAT registration: 291 8753 42

Date/tax point: 9 March 1998

Invoice to:
Polycot Limited
17 Hightown Road
Branston BN4 3EW

Invoice number: 2115

Your order: 3912

Item description	Quantity	Unit price £	Trade discount @ 30% £	Net price £	Total £
Plastic poppers (100 in each box)	100 boxes	92.00	27.60	64.40	6,440.00
Total					6,440.00
VAT @ 17.5%					1,127.00
Total due					7,567.00
Terms: net 30 days					

SALES INVOICE

Hartston Limited
55 Parlour Street, Jamestown, FE6 8UR
Telephone: 01225 67124

VAT registration: 214 5143 28

Date/tax point: 12 March 1998

Invoice to:
Polycot Limited
17 Hightown Road
Branston BN4 3EW

Invoice number: 34415

Your order: 3932

Item description	Quantity	Unit price £	Trade discount @ 30% £	Net price £	Total £
Plastic poppers (100 in each box)	100 boxes	95.00	28.50	66.50	6,650.00
Total					6,650.00
VAT @ 17.5%					1,163.75
Total due					7,813.75
Terms: net 30 days					

SALES INVOICE

Baxter Limited
39 Langdale Avenue, Bisham MW3 9TY
Telephone: 01693 77612

VAT registration: 215 8761 34

Date/tax point: 12 March 1998

Invoice to:
Polycot Limited
17 Hightown Road
Branston BN4 3EW

Invoice number: 7249

Your order: 3917

Item description	**Quantity**	**Unit price £**	**Trade discount @ 30% £**	**Net price £**	**Total £**
Cotton - 50 metre rolls	90	126.00	37.80	88.20	7,938.00
Total					7,938.00
VAT @ 17.5%					1,389.15
Total due					9,327.15

Terms: net 30 days

MATERIALS REQUISITION

DATE *6 March 1998* NUMBER *944*

DEPARTMENT *Finishing*

QUANTITY	CODE	DESCRIPTION
90	*PP29*	*Plastic poppers*

SIGNATURE *Jim Stubbs*

MATERIALS REQUISITION

DATE *10 March 1998* **NUMBER** *948*

DEPARTMENT *Cutting*

QUANTITY	CODE	DESCRIPTION
50	*CT33*	*Cotton, 50 metre rolls*

SIGNATURE *Jim Stubbs*

MATERIALS REQUISITION

DATE *18 March 1998* **NUMBER** *959*

DEPARTMENT *Cutting*

QUANTITY	CODE	DESCRIPTION
40	*CT33*	*Cotton, 50 metre rolls*

SIGNATURE *Jim Stubbs*

MATERIALS REQUISITION		
DATE *20 March 1998*		NUMBER *961*
DEPARTMENT *Finishing*		
QUANTITY	**CODE**	**DESCRIPTION**
110	*PP29*	*Plastic poppers*
SIGNATURE *Jim Stubbs*		

MATERIALS REQUISITION		
DATE *30 March 1998*		NUMBER *984*
DEPARTMENT *Cutting*		
QUANTITY	**CODE**	**DESCRIPTION**
30	*C733*	*Cotton, 50 metre rolls*
SIGNATURE *Jim Stubbs*		

INTERNAL POLICY DOCUMENT

Document no. 15
Subject: Wages
Issued: December 1997

Direct labour rates to be paid

Employee grade	£ per hour
1	4.00
2	3.00
3	2.50

The above rates are also payable for any hours spent on indirect work.

Direct employees work an eight hour day.

Overtime (any hours worked in excess of eight per day): employees are to be paid for one and a half hours for every hour of overtime that they work.

Employees will be paid a bonus of £0.15 for every duvet cover produced in excess of 60 in any single day. No in lieu bonuses are paid for idle time, training etc.

Employees are to be credited with eight hours for any full days when they are sick, on holiday, or engaged in training activities. Half or part days are credited on a pro rata basis. These hours are to be paid at the basic rate.

Analysis of wages

The following are to be treated as direct labour costs:

* Payment for hours spent on direct tasks
* The basic pay for overtime spent on direct tasks

The following are to be treated as indirect labour costs:

* Overtime premium payments
* Bonus payments
* Idle time payments
* Holiday pay, sick pay and training pay

Discrepancies on time sheets

The company wishes to facilitate the prompt payment of wages and early reporting of labour costs to management. Employees will initially be paid for the total number of hours shown at the bottom of their time sheet, plus appropriate bonuses and overtime premiums.

Any discrepancies on time sheets are to be temporarily adjusted within direct labour hours, pending the outcome of enquiries.

Production overheads for the year to 31 March 1999

Polycot Ltd rents its production premises. The rent and rates for the year to 31 March 1999 will amount to £79,500.

Catering facilities for production staff are limited to a number of vending machines dispensing drinks and snacks. The rent for these machines during the year ending 31 March 1999 will be £100 per month.

Machinery and equipment owned by Polycot is subject to a maintenance contract covering preventive and urgent maintenance, parts, labour and call out charges. For the year to 31 March 1999 the maintenance company will charge £25,250 in respect of the machinery in the cutting department, £5,600 in respect of machinery in the finishing department, £11,000 in respect of machinery in the packing department and £4,000 in respect of machinery in the stores department. Depreciation on all machinery will total £13,490.

The production manager's salary will be £21,000 for the year; he divides his time about equally between the three production departments. The storekeeper's salary will be £14,000.

Other production overheads for the year are estimated at £40,000. The general manager has suggested that this cost should be divided evenly across the four departments.

The following data is also available.

	Cutting	Finishing	Packing	Stores
Floor area (sq metres)	1,900	2,650	1,900	1,125
Number of employees	20	68	40	3
Cost of machinery	£74,125	£16,625	£32,300	£11,850
Direct labour hours	5,125	129,750	67,500	
Machine hours	30,750	28,350	10,750	
Number of materials requisitions	21,175	17,675	14,100	

MEMO

To: Lesley Hunt
From: Patrick McGrath, General Manager
Date: 3 July 1998
Subject: Overhead absorption, quarter ending 30 June 1998

Your colleague in the accounts department had almost completed the task of calculating the production overheads under or over absorbed for the last quarter. Unfortunately she was not able to complete the task before leaving for her summer holiday. She has asked me to pass on the following information, and assures me that you will know what to do in order to complete the calculations.

Thanks for your help.

Information attached to the memo:

Amounts charged to cost centre code C300 - Packing department: quarter ending 30 June 1998

Cost centre code	*Expenditure code*	*Amount charged* £
C300	E200	8,020
C300	E210	855
C300	E300	48,345
C300	E310	4,045
C300	E410	10,800
C300	E500	800

Labour hours analysis - quarter ending 30 June 1998

	Cutting department hours	*Finishing department* hours	*Packing department* hours
Direct labour hours	1,200	38,800	18,300
Indirect labour hours	890	1,250	1,830
Total labour hours	2,090	40,050	20,130

Note. The above tables do not include a payment that I still have to enquire about, as follows.

- Wages paid to temporary employee for 320 hours worked during the quarter ending 30 June 1998: £1,920.

Standard costs for 1998/99

The general manager, Patrick McGrath, has informed you of the following decisions relating to standard costs for double duvet covers for the year ending 31 March 1999.

Cotton prices

Assume a 5 per cent increase over the highest price paid in March 1998. (Refer back to the relevant stores ledger card for this information.)

Plastic poppers

Assume a price of £67 per box of 100.

Thread

Assume a price of £14.20 per 10,000 metres.

Packing cartons

Assume a price of £0.25 per box, each box being large enough for 6 double covers.

Direct labour

Assume a 5 per cent increase over current rates for all grades.

MEMO

To: Lesley Hunt
From: Patrick McGrath
Date: 12 July 1998
Subject: Standard cost report for double duvet covers in Cutting department

I have collated some of the data you will need for the standard cost report for week ended 8 July - see below.

Please could you let me have an analysis of all the cost variances that you can calculate from this, with explanations of any significant ones. I'd be grateful if you could let me have this by close of business tomorrow.

Cost data for week ended 8 July 1998 - double duvet covers in Cutting department

Output
Budgeted double covers produced in the week = 1,900; actual double covers produced in the week = 1,760.

Materials
Cotton used = 11,350 metres, costing £21,565.

Direct labour
Cutting department = 90 hours of Grade 1 labour, costing £402.

Machine hours
Cutting department = 560 machine hours

Overhead
Production overhead charged to Cutting department = £1,650.

AAT SAMPLE SIMULATION

Recording Cost Information

ANSWER BOOKLET

Task 1

STORES LEDGER ACCOUNT

Material description: *Plastic poppers, boxes of 100*

Code no: *PP29*

Maximum quantity: *180*
Minimum quantity: *62*
Reorder level: *95*
Reorder quantity: *100*

Date	Receipts			Issues			Stock balance		
	Quantity	Price per box £	Total £	Quantity	Price per box £	Total £	Quantity	Price per box £	Total £
1 March							*75*	*62.50*	*4,687.50*

STORES LEDGER ACCOUNT

Material description: *Cotton, 50m rolls*

Code no: *C733*

Maximum quantity: *175*
Minimum quantity: *55*
Reorder level: *75*
Reorder quantity: *90*

Date	Receipts			Issues			Stock balance		
	Quantity	Price per roll £	Total £	Quantity	Price per roll £	Total £	Quantity	Price per roll £	Total £
1 March							*65*	*85.50*	*5,557.50*

Task 2

MEMO

To: Patrick McGrath
From: Lesley [illegible]
Date: 3.4.98
Subject: Stores Ledger Account

On looking at the Stores Ledger card for this month I note the follow matter which I feel you should be aware of

<u>Plastic Poppers</u>

On the 12th it was over the maximum quantity. The order of 100 on the 12th shouldn't have happened the re-order level [illegible] at 98.

<u>Cotten 5cm Rolls</u>

On the 12th this also was over the maximum quantity level.

I will speak to the the stores worker and deal with this matter

Lesley

BPP PUBLISHING

Task 3

TIMESHEET

Week ending *6 March 1998*

Employee name *Amy Harding* **Employee number** *2173*

Department *Finishing* **Employee grade** *2*

Activity	**Monday** Hours	**Tuesday** Hours	**Wednesday** Hours	**Thursday** Hours	**Friday** Hours	**Total** Hours
Machining	7	10	4		4	
Holiday			4	8		
Waiting for work	1					
Training					4	
Total hours payable for day	8	10	8	8	8	
Number of covers produced	65	72	30	0	32	
Bonus payable @ £0.15 per cover above 60 per day						

Signed *Amy Harding* **Manager** *Jim Stubbs*

Analysis for week	**Hours**	**Rate per hour** £	**Wages cost** £
Direct wages			
Indirect wages			
Basic hours			
Overtime premium			
Bonus			

Task 3, continued

TIMESHEET

Week ending *6 March 1998*

Employee name	*Jane Amber*	**Employee number**	*2487*
Department	*Cutting*	**Employee grade**	*1*

Activity	**Monday** Hours	**Tuesday** Hours	**Wednesday** Hours	**Thursday** Hours	**Friday** Hours	**Total** Hours
Cutting	*10*	*6*	*6*		*8*	
Waiting for work		*3*	*2*			
Sick				*8*		
Training					*2*	
Total hours payable for day	*10*	*8*	*8*	*8*	*10*	
Number of covers produced	*70*	*51*	*62*	*0*	*62*	
Bonus payable @ £0.15 per cover above 60 per day						

Signed	*Jane Amber*	**Manager**	*Jim Stubbs*

Analysis for week	**Hours**	**Rate per hour** £	**Wages cost** £
Direct wages			
Indirect wages			
Basic hours			
Overtime premium			
Bonus			

Task 3, continued

COST LEDGER DATA ENTRY SHEET

Week ending

Debit accounts

Cost centre code	Expenditure code	Amount to be debited £
C100	E300	
C200	E300	
C300	E300	
C400	E300	
C100	E310	
C200	E310	
C300	E310	
C400	E310	

Check total: total wages for the two employees

Task 4

MEMO

To:
From:
Date:
Subject:

Task 5

MEMO

To: Jim Stubbs

From: Lesley H[illegible]

Date: 10-3-98

Subject: Overhead [illegible]

As you are [illegible] absorbs all production overheads [illegible] hrs.

The company [illegible] machine hrs [illegible] department.

[illegible] the Cutting D[illegible] intensive [illegible] machine [illegible]

[illegible] to keep [illegible]

Task 6

OVERHEAD ANALYSIS SHEET: 1998/99						
Overhead expense: primary apportionments and allocations	**Basis of allocation/ apportionment**	**Total** **£**	**Cutting dept** **£**	**Finishing dept** **£**	**Packing dept** **£**	**Stores** **£**
Total of primary allocations						
Re-apportion stores						
Total production cost centre overhead						
Machine hours						
Direct labour hours						
Overhead absorption rate for 1998/99						

Task 7a

MEMO

To:
From:
Date:
Subject:

Task 7b, c, d

Working sheet for calculation of overhead under/over absorbed

Packing department, quarter ending 30 June 1998

7(b) Production overhead absorbed	£
7(c) Actual production overhead incurred	£
7(d) Production overhead under or over absorbed, to be transferred to profit and loss account	£

Task 8

STANDARD COST CARD 1998/99				
Product: Box of 6 double duvet covers Product code no: 00214				
Description	**Material code no/direct labour grade**	**Quantity**	**Std price** £ per metre/ hour etc	**Total** £
Direct materials				
Cotton fabric	CT33	38.2 metres	1.85	70.67
Plastic poppers	PP29	60	67.00	40.20
Polyester thread	TP72	22 metres	14.20	0.03
Packing - cardboard box	PB03	1 box	0.25	0.25
Other materials	Various	-	-	0.81
Subtotal, direct materials			(A)	111.96
Direct labour				
Cutting	Grade 1	0.35 hours	4.00	1.40
Finishing	Grade 1	4.10 hours	4.00	16.40
Packing	Grade 3	0.50 hours	2.50	1.25
Subtotal, direct labour			(B)	19.05
Production overhead				
Cutting department		1.80 machine hours	2.80	5.04
Finishing department		4.10 labour hours	0.51	2.09
Packing department		0.50 labour hours	0.93	0.46
Subtotal, production overhead			(C)	7.59
Total standard production cost			(A + B + C)	138.60

Task 9

MEMO

To:
From:
Date:
Subject:

Workings

Trial run central assessments

TRIAL RUN CENTRAL ASSESSMENT 1

INTERMEDIATE STAGE - NVQ/SVQ3

Unit 6

Recording Cost Information
June 2000

This Central Assessment is in TWO sections. You are reminded that competence must be achieved in both sections. You should therefore attempt and aim to complete EVERY task in BOTH sections.

NOTE: All essential calculations should be included within your answers where appropriate.

You are advised to spend 1 hour 30 minutes on each section.

SECTION 1

You are advised to spend approximately 1 hour 30 minutes on this section.

Data

You work as an accounting technician at the Langley Hotel which is part of a large group of hotels. It is your task each month to record and report cost information to Head Office.

The Langley Hotel has thirty bedrooms and its operations are organised into five cost centres.

These are:

- Accommodation
- Restaurant
- Bar
- Kitchen
- Administration

The management team consists of:

- General manager
- Head waiter
- Bar manager
- Chef

Data

The bar manager purchases wines from a number of suppliers. The best selling wine is 'New World Red' which is ordered weekly. Stock records for all wines show both actual and standard cost and identify any price variance at the time of receipt. Stocks are valued at standard cost. The standard cost of a single bottle of 'New World Red' is £5.

Task 1.1

Complete the stock card for 'New World Red' for the four weeks ended 28 May 2000.

STOCK CARD								
Product:								
	Receipts					**Issues**	**Balance**	
Date	**Quantity**	**Actual Cost (per bottle)** £	**Total Actual Cost** £	**Total Standard Cost** £	**Price Variance** £	**Quantity**	**Quantity**	**Total Standard Cost** £
B/f at 1 May	100			500.00			100	500.00
2 May	240	5.20	1,248.00	1,200.00	48.00		340	1,700.00
7 May						300		
9 May	180	5.30						
14 May						200		
16 May	360	5.00						
21 May						230		
23 May	480	4.95						
28 May						120		

Task 1.2

Calculate the total price variance for 'New World Red' for the four weeks ended 28 May 2000.

....

....

....

....

Task 1.3

Calculate the value of stocks of 'New World Red' at 28 May 2000 if they were valued on an actual cost basis using the First-In-First-Out (FIFO) method.

Data

Some stock issues of 'New World Red' are made, at standard cost, to the kitchen where the wine is used as an ingredient in preparing evening meals. The standard quantity used in preparing ten evening meals is one bottle. During the four weeks ended 28 May 2000, the kitchen prepared 1,500 evening meals and used 100 bottles of wine.

Task 1.4

Calculate the usage variance of 'New World Red' for the four weeks ended 28 May 2000.

Data

The following information relates to the kitchen.

- The standard time to prepare an evening meal is 20 minutes.
- The standard time to prepare a breakfast meal is 10 minutes.
- The kitchen employs five staff including the chef.
- The average wage rate is £6 per hour.
- All kitchen staff are directly involved in preparing meals.

Actual data for the four weeks ended 28 May 2000 are as follows:

- 1,500 evening meals prepared
- 1,380 breakfast meals prepared
- 800 hours worked
- £5,000 wages paid

Task 1.5

This task consists of parts (a) - (e)

(a) Calculate the total standard labour time in hours to prepare the actual number of evening meals and breakfast meals for the four weeks ended 28 May 2000.

(b) Calculate the total standard labour cost for the actual number of evening meals and breakfast meals prepared for the four weeks ended 28 May 2000.

(c) Calculate the total labour cost variance for the four weeks ended 28 May 2000.

(d) Calculate the labour efficiency variance.

(e) Calculate the labour wage rate variance.

Task 1.6

Using the information from tasks 1.2, 1.4 and 1.5 you are required to:

- Complete the standard cost report below
- Comment on possible causes for each of the variances

STANDARD DIRECT COST REPORT (EXTRACT) Period:		
Description	**Favourable Variance** **£**	**Adverse Variance** **£**
BAR		
'New World Red' price variance		
KITCHEN		
'New World Red' usage variance		
Labour efficiency variance		
Labour wage rate variance		

COMMENTS

SECTION 2

You are advised to spend approximately 1 hour 30 minutes on this section.

Data

The budgeted overheads for the Langley Hotel are all treated as fixed costs. The budget for a four week period is as follows:

	£
Bedroom repairs	2,400
Electricity	1,350
Rent	12,000
Kitchen repairs	580
Staff costs: accommodation	2,200
restaurant	4,200
bar	1,500
kitchen	-
administration	5,210
Other property overheads	2,800
	32,240

The following information is also relevant:

Cost centre	Percentage of floor space occupied	Metered electricity costs
		£
Accommodation	60%	450
Restaurant	20%	200
Bar	10%	50
Kitchen	5%	600
Administration	5%	50
	100%	1,350

Overheads are allocated and apportioned to the five cost centres using the most appropriate method. The total administration overheads are then reapportioned to the other four cost centres using the following percentages:

- Accommodation 70%
- Restaurant 10%
- Bar 10%
- Kitchen 10%

Task 2.1

Complete the table below showing:

- The basis for allocation or apportionment of each overhead
- The allocation and apportionment of budgeted overheads between the five cost centres
- The reapportionment of the total administration overheads

Overhead	Basis	Total £	Accommodation £	Restaurant £	Bar £	Kitchen £	Administration £
Bedroom repairs	Allocated	2,400.00	2,400.00				
Electricity		1,350.00					
Rent		12,000.00					
Kitchen repairs		580.00					
Staff costs		13,110.00					
Other property overheads		2,800.00					
		32,240.00					
Administration							
		32,240.00					

Data

The staff budget for the kitchen assumes:

- 5 staff for 2 hours each morning prepare breakfast meals;
- 5 staff for 4 hours each evening prepare evening meals;
- breakfast meals and evening meals are prepared every day.

Task 2.2

Calculate the budgeted number of direct labour hours to be worked in the kitchen during a four week period.

Task 2.3

Using your results from tasks 2.1 and 2.2, calculate the budgeted labour hour overhead absorption rate for the kitchen.

Data

Each breakfast meal is budgeted to take 10 minutes to prepare and each evening meal takes 20 minutes. For cost accounting, kitchen overheads are absorbed using a direct labour hour basis to calculate the full cost of a breakfast meal and evening meal.

Task 2.4

Using your answer from task 2.3, calculate the overhead cost for each meal.

Data

As stated in task 1.5, actual data for the kitchen, for the four weeks ended 28 May 2000, are as follows:

- 1,500 evening meals prepared; 1500 × £1 1500
- 1,380 breakfast meals prepared; 1380 × 50p 690
- 800 hours worked. 2190 2520

In addition, an analysis of actual overheads for the four weeks ended 28 May 2000 shows that the actual overhead for the kitchen is £2,100.

Actual 2,100
budget 2520
420

Task 2.5

Complete the standard cost report below and then comment on possible causes for each of the variances.

STANDARD INDIRECT COST REPORT		
Cost centre: kitchen **Period:** 4 weeks ended 28 May 2000.		
Description	**Favourable Variance** **£**	**Adverse Variance** **£**
Fixed overhead expenditure variance	420	
Fixed overhead volume variance		330
Fixed overhead capacity variance		120
Fixed overhead efficiency variance		210

COMMENTS

fixed o/H expenditure Variance
Actual o/H 2,100
Budget " 2520
420
fixed o/H Volume Variance
1,500 meals produced × £1 = 1500
1 380 Breakfast " × 50p " = 690
2190
2520
330(A)
fixed o/H capacity Variance
Actual hours worked 800
stand time 840
40 A × £3 = 120(A)
fixed o/H Efficiency
70 hr A × £3 = £210.

TRIAL RUN CENTRAL ASSESSMENT 2

INTERMEDIATE STAGE - NVQ/SVQ3

Unit 6

Recording Cost Information

December 2000

This Central Assessment is in two sections. You are reminded that competence must be achieved in both sections. You should therefore attempt and aim to complete EVERY task in BOTH sections.

Essential calculations should be included within your answers where appropriate.

You are advised to spend 1 hour 30 minutes on each section.

Both sections of this Central Assessment are based on Mobiles Ltd. Data provided in Section 1 may also be required for Section 2.

SECTION 1

You are advised to spend approximately 1 hour 30 minutes on this section.

Data

You work as an accounting technician at Mobiles Ltd, a company which assembles a range of telephones from plastic casings and printed circuit boards.

The company is organised into four departments as follows:

- Assembly
- Stores
- Sales
- Administration

The standard direct cost of the company's main product, the S100 model, for the month ended 30 November 2000 was as follows:

Product: S100			
Direct materials	**Quantity**	**Unit price** £	**Total Cost** £
Plastic casing	1	6.00	6.00
Printed circuit boards ('PCBs')	2	4.50	9.00
Direct labour	**Hours**	**Hourly rate**	
Assembly labour	0.25	£4.00	1.00
			16.00

Printed circuit boards (PCBs) for the S100 model are purchased only from Electronics Ltd. An analysis of purchase invoices from this supplier for November 2000 revealed the following information:

Date of invoice	**Quantity of PCBs**	**Unit price** £	**Total price** £
2.11.2000	10,000	5.50	55,000.00
9.11.2000	8,500	6.00	51,000.00
16.11.2000	20,000	4.50	90,000.00
23.11.2000	18,000	5.00	90,000.00
30.11.2000	15,000	5.00	75,000.00

The company records stocks of materials at standard cost. Stocks of PCBs were as follows:

- At 1 November 35,000 PCBs
- At 30 November 32,000 PCBs

The stock record for the S100 model for November 2000 shows:

- 35,000 units were produced
- 30,000 units were sold
- At 30 November stocks totalled 7,000 units

Task 1.1

Calculate the total price variance for PCBs for November 2000.

Task 1.2

Calculate the standard usage of PCBs for the total production of the S100 model for November 2000.

Task 1.3

Calculate the actual usage of PCBs and the total usage variance for PCBs for November 2000.

Additional Data

The company's production budget for 2001 requires 8,000 units of the S100 model to be assembled each week. The company plans to maintain a buffer stock of PCBs for the S100 model equivalent to one week's budgeted production. Electronics Ltd can take between one and two weeks to deliver PCBs that have been ordered.

Task 1.4

Calculate the buffer stock level and the reorder level for PCBs.

Additional Data

An analysis of the payroll for the assembly department for November 2000 is as follows:

Assembly Department	Hours worked	Gross Cost £
Direct labour:		
for the S100 model	8,250	38,775.00
for all other models	5,600	22,400.00
Indirect labour	560	5,600.00

Task 1.5

This task consists of parts (a) – (e).

Calculate for the S100 model for November 2000:

(a) **the standard labour time to assemble total production:**

(b) **the standard labour cost for total production:**

(c) **the total labour cost variance:**

(d) **the labour efficiency variance:**

....

....

....

(e) **the labour wage rate variance:**

....

....

....

Task 1.6

Using the information from tasks 1.1 – 1.5, complete the standard cost report as follows.

- **Insert the variances.**
- **Explain the significance of each variance for the procedures in establishing standard material and labour costs for the S100 model for the year 2001.**
- **Explain the terms basic cost standards, ideal cost standards and current attainable cost standards**

STANDARD DIRECT COST REPORT (EXTRACT)

Period: November 2000

Description	**Favourable Variance (£)**	**Adverse Variance (£)**
PCB price variance		
PCB usage variance		
S100 labour efficiency variance		
S100 labour wage rate variance		

SECTION 2

You are advised to spend approximately 1 hour 30 minutes on this section.

You are reminded that data from Section 1 may also be required in this section.

Additional Data

Assembly department overheads at Mobiles Ltd are charged to products at a predetermined overhead absorption rate based on budgeted direct labour hours. Set out below are the budgeted and actual overheads for the assembly department for November 2000. These have all been treated as fixed overheads.

Task 2.1

Complete the table below showing the expenditure variance for each overhead cost.

	Actual £	**Budget** £	**Variance** £
Supervisors' wages	5,600	5,200	
Rent and rates	24,400	24,000	
Buildings insurance	2,850	3,000	
Power	7,240	6,800	
Heat and light	6,250	6,000	
Consumable materials	22,160	18,750	
Depreciation of machinery	30,000	30,000	
Total	98,500	93,750	

Additional Data

The following data relates to the assembly department for November 2000:

	Number of hours
• Budgeted direct labour hours	12,500
• Actual direct labour hours	13,850
• Standard direct labour hours for actual production	12,200

Task 2.2

This task consists of parts (a) – (d).

Calculate for the assembly department for November 2000:

(a) the budgeted direct labour hour overhead absorption rate:

....

....

....

(b) the overhead volume variance:

....

....

....

....

(c) **the overhead efficiency variance:**

Standard ....

Actual ....

....

....

(d) **the overhead capacity variance:**

....

....

....

....

Additional Data

The company operates an integrated cost accounting system in which all finished goods stocks are valued at standard absorption cost.

Task 2.3

This task consists of parts (a) and (b).

(a) **Prepare the journal entry for the absorption of assembly department overheads for November 2000 for inclusion in the cost accounting records:**

	Dr £	Cr £
Finished goods stocks 12,200 x £7.50		
Fixed overhead expenditure variance		
Fixed overhead volume variance		
Fixed overhead control – assembly		

(b) **Explain how the fixed overhead expenditure and volume variances will be dealt with in the management accounts for November 2000.**

....

....

....

....

....

....

....

....

....

....

....

....

Additional Data

The Managing Director has asked you to prepare the budgeted overhead costs for January 2001 using the actual cost information and actual labour hours for November 2000 as a base. You should compute the overheads for two budgeted activity levels, 14,000 direct labour hours and 15,000 direct labour hours. All overheads are treated as fixed except for consumable materials which are treated as variable with direct labour hours.

Task 2.4

Complete the budgeted overhead cost schedule below for the different levels of activity.

	NOVEMBER RESULTS	**BUDGETED ACTIVITY (Direct labour hours)**	
Direct labour hours	13,850	14,000	15,000
	Base cost	**Budgeted cost**	**Budgeted cost**
	£	**£**	**£**
Supervisors' wages	5,600		
Rent and rates	24,400		
Buildings insurance	2,850		
Power	7,240		
Heat and light	6,250		
Consumable materials	22,160		
Depreciation of machinery	30,000		
Total	**98,500**		

Task 2.5

Explain the effect of an increase in activity level on the overhead cost to be charged to an individual product.

Task 2.6

The Managing Director has asked you to draft a report explaining the significance of the information in tasks 2.1 – 2.5 to the process of setting the standard fixed overhead absorption rate for the forthcoming year.

REPORT

To:

From:

Subject:

Date:

TRIAL RUN CENTRAL ASSESSMENT 3

INTERMEDIATE STAGE - NVQ/SVQ3

Unit 6

Recording Cost Information
June 2001

This central assessment is in TWO sections. You have to show competence in BOTH sections. You should therefore attempt and aim to complete EVERY task in BOTH sections. You should spend about 90 minutes on each section.

All essential calculations should be included within your answers, where appropriate.

Both sections are based on Roman Ltd. Data provided in Section 1 may also be needed for Section 2.

SECTION 1

You should spend about 90 minutes on this section.

Data

Roman Ltd sells and services cars. You work as an accounting technician at Roman Ltd and report to the Finance Director.

The company operates an integrated cost accounting system. For the servicing department this involves you:

- calculating motor oil material price variances at the time of purchase;
- recording purchases and issues of motor oil at the standard cost of £1 per litre.

The Finance Director has given you the following tasks.

Task 1.1

Complete the following stock card for motor oil for May 2001.

STOCK CARD

Product: **Motor oil**
Standard price: **£1 per litre**
Centre: **Servicing**

	Receipts					Issues	Balance	
Date	**Quantity**	**Actual cost per litre**	**Total actual cost**	**Total standard cost**	**Price variance**	**Quantity**	**Quantity**	**Total standard cost**
	litres	£	£	£	£	litres	litres	£
B/f 1 May							2,100	2,100
4 May	2,400	1.20	2,880	2,400	480		4,500	4,500
8 May						3,300		
10 May	3,000	1.10						
11 May						3,200		
17 May	5,000	1.00						
18 May						5,400		
23 May	6,400	0.95						
24 May						4,420		

Task 1.2

Calculate the total material price variance for purchases of motor oil for May 2001.

Task 1.3

(a) Prepare the journal entry to record the purchase of motor oil in May.

	Dr	Cr
	£	£
Motor oil stocks		
Material price variance		
Creditors' control account		

(b) Explain how you should record the material price variance balance in the profit and loss account for the month ended 31 May 2001.

Additional data

Roman Ltd services many different types of car.

The standard direct cost of an oil service for a car, no matter what engine size, is as follows.

			Total cost
Direct materials	**Quantity**	**Unit price**	£
Motor oil	10 litres	£1.00	10.00
Direct labour	**Hours**	**Hourly rate**	
Mechanic	0.75	£10.00	7.50
			17.50

An analysis of the time sheets of mechanics for May shows:

- number of oil services completed was 1,420;
- time spent carrying out oil services was 1,250 hours;
- total labour cost for carrying out oil services was £10,850;
- actual usage of motor oil used in servicing cars was 16,320 litres.

Task 1.4

Calculate for the total number of oil services for May 2001:

(a) the standard usage of motor oil

(b) the material usage variance for motor oil

(c) the standard labour time

(d) the standard labour cost

(e) the labour efficiency variance

(f) the labour rate variance

Additional data

The company charges direct labour costs to cost of sales at standard cost. Labour variances are then separately identified.

Task 1.5

(a) Prepare the journal entry for May 2001 for labour costs relating to oil services.

	Dr	Cr
	£	£
Cost of sales		
Labour efficiency variance		
Labour rate variance		
Wages control account		

(b) Explain how you should record the labour rate variance and labour efficiency variance balances in the profit and loss account for the month ended 31 May 2001.

Task 1.6

Using the blank stationery on the next two pages, prepare a report. Your report should:

(a) use the data given in task 1.1 to suggest ONE possible reason for the material price variance;

(b) use the data given in task 1.4 to suggest ONE possible reason for the material usage variance;

(c) suggest ONE possible reason for the labour rate variance;

(d) suggest ONE possible reason for the labour efficiency variance.

REPORT

To: **Finance Director** **From:**

Subject: **Date:**

Task 1.6, continued

REPORT

SECTION 2

You should spend about 90 minutes on this section.

Additional data

Roman Ltd organises its operations into three profit centres and one cost centre, as follows.

Profit centres

- New car sales
- Used car sales
- Servicing

Cost centre

- Administration

The budgeted overheads of the company are all treated as fixed costs. The monthly budgeted overheads are as follows.

	£
Depreciation	7,200
Rent	20,000
Other property overheads	11,500
Fixed staff costs - new car sales	62,100
used car sales	54,200
servicing	28,200
administration	25,210
Administration overheads	25,840
Total monthly budgeted fixed overheads	234,250

The following information is also relevant.

Profit/cost centre	**% of floor space occupied**	**Net book value of fixed assets**
	%	£'000
New car sales	40	60
Used car sales	30	60
Servicing	20	200
Administration	10	40
	100	360

Overheads are allocated and apportioned using the most appropriate method. The total administration overheads are then reapportioned to the three profit centres using the following percentages.

Apportionment of administration overheads

New car sales	20%
Used car sales	30%
Servicing	50%

Task 2.1

Complete the table below showing:

- the basis for allocation or apportionment of each overhead;
- the allocation and apportionment of budgeted overheads between the four centres;
- the reapportionment of the total administration overheads.

Fixed overhead	Basis	Total	New car sales	Used car sales	Servicing	Administration
		£	£	£	£	£
Depreciation		7,200				
Rent		20,000				
Other property overheads		11,500				
Fixed staff costs		169,710				
Administration overheads		25,840				
		234,250				
Administration						( )
		234,250				

Additional data

Servicing centre fixed overheads are absorbed on the basis of budgeted direct labour hours. For the servicing centre for May 2001:

- the budgeted number of direct labour hours was 8,250 hours;
- time sheets show that 8,500 direct labour hours were worked;
- output represented 8,100 standard hours;
- actual fixed overheads were £72,540.

Task 2.2

Calculate for May 2001 for the servicing centre:

(a) the standard fixed overhead absorption rate per direct labour hour

....

....

....

....

(b) the fixed overhead expenditure variance

....

....

....

....

(c) the fixed overhead volume variance

....

....

....

....

(d) the fixed overhead efficiency variance

....

....

....

....

(e) the fixed overhead capacity variance

....

....

....

....

Additional data

The company is considering expanding its servicing activities. It has two choices:

- increase direct labour hours by 10%;
- increase direct labour hours by 20%.

An increase in activity is expected to increase budgeted overheads for servicing operations as follows.

- 'other property overheads' will increase by £4,000 per month **if there is any increase** in activities;
- additional plant and machinery costing £84,000 will be required **if activity is increased by more than 10%**. Plant and machinery is depreciated over five years assuming no residual values and using the straight line method of depreciation.

Task 2.3

Complete the table overleaf for the servicing centre showing:

(a) budgeted overheads for May 2001 (from task 2.1);

(b) budgeted overheads for each activity level;

(c) the standard fixed overhead absorption rate per direct labour hour for each activity level.

Servicing	**Budgeted activity (labour hours)** 8,250	9,075	9,900
Budgeted fixed overheads	**May 2001** £	£	£
Depreciation			
Rent			
Other property overheads			
Staff costs			
Administration			
Total			
Standard overhead absorption rate (rounded to nearest penny)			

Task 2.4

The Finance Director is concerned about the effect of the current level of costs on profitability.

He asks you to:

(a) provide the budgeted overhead cost for an oil service for each of the activity levels described in task 2.3. You answer should be rounded to the nearest penny.

Activity level	£
8,250 labour hours	
9,075 labour hours	
9,900 labour hours	

(b) calculate, to one decimal place

(i) the efficiency ratio; and
(ii) the capacity ratio

for the servicing centre for May 2001.

....

....

....

....

....

....

....

....

....

....

Task 2.5

Company records show that the fixed overhead cost of an oil change is £6. Using the blank stationery below, prepare a report which BRIEFLY explains:

(a) how the £6 fixed overhead cost of an oil change was calculated;

(b) how the fixed overhead expenditure variance calculated in task 2.2 might be used to revise the standard fixed overhead absorption rates;

(c) the effect of the changes in activity calculated in task 2.3 on standard fixed overhead absorption rates;

(d) the meaning of the fixed overhead capacity and efficiency ratios calculated in task 2.4.

REPORT

To: Finance Director	**From:**
Subject:	**Date:**

DECEMBER 2001 CENTRAL ASSESSMENT

INTERMEDIATE STAGE - NVQ/SVQ3

Unit 6

Recording Cost Information

This Central Assessment is in TWO sections.

You have to show competence in BOTH sections.

You should therefore attempt and aim to complete EVERY task in BOTH sections.

All essential calculations should be included within your answers where appropriate.

SECTION 1

You are advised to spend about 90 minutes on this section.

Data

Design Ltd manufactures and sells furnishing fabrics. You work as an accounting technician at Design Ltd, reporting to the finance director.

All furnishing fabrics are manufactured using white cloth which is dyed and printed. White cloth is purchased from a number of suppliers. The company operates a standard cost stock system.

- White cloth has a standard cost of £2.20 per metre.
- All price variances are recorded on receipt of the purchase invoice.

The finance director has given you the following tasks.

Task 1.1

Complete the following stock card for white cloth for November 2001.

STOCK CARD

Product: White cloth

Standard cost: £2.20 per metre

	Receipts					Issues	Balance	
Date	**Quantity** Metres	**Actual Cost (per metre)** £	**Total Actual Cost** £	**Total Standard Cost** £	**Price Variance** £	**Quantity** Metres	**Quantity** Metres	**Total Standard Cost** £
B/f at 1 Nov							60,200	132,440
4 Nov	11,400	2.50	28,500	25,080	3,420		71,600	157,520
8 Nov						24,800		
10 Nov	13,000	2.40						
11 Nov						18,200		
17 Nov	15,200	2.30						
18 Nov						15,400		
23 Nov	16,600	2.25						
30 Nov						24,480		

Task 1.2

Calculate the total price variance for white cloth for November 2001.

....

....

....

....

....

....

Data

The standard cost card for **100 metres** of *Rosy Glow* fabric is shown below.

STANDARD COST CARD			
Product: Rosy Glow			
Standard cost: 100 metres			
Inputs	**Quantity**	**Unit price (£)**	**Standard cost per 100 metres (£)**
Direct material			
White cloth	101 metres	2.20	222.20
Red dye	10 litres	8.00	80.00
Direct labour	5 hours	6.00	30.00
Standard cost per 100 metres			332.20

Actual data for the month of November

Production of Rosy Glow	8,500 metres
White cloth used	9,000 metres
Red dye used	900 litres
Direct labour hours worked	550 hours
Hourly wage rate paid	£5.25

Task 1.3

This task consists of parts (a) to (h).

Calculate for the manufacture of Rosy Glow for November 2001:

(a) the standard usage of white cloth;

....

....

....

(b) the standard usage of red dye;

....

....

....

(c) the material usage variance for white cloth;

Actual Usage 9,000 metre

should have used 8,585

415 metres (A)

× 2.20 = £913 (A)

(d) the material usage variance for red dye;

Actual Usage 850 litre

should have used 900 "

50 (F)

× £8 = £400 (F)

(e) the standard labour time;

5 hrs / 100 metre = 0.05 × 8,500 = 425 hrs

(f) the standard labour cost;

425 hrs × £6 hrs = £2,550

(g) the labour efficiency variance;

Actual 550

Should 425

125 (A)

× £6

£750 (A)

(h) the labour rate variance

Actual 550 hr x £5.25 = 2,887.50

Should 550 x £6 = 3300.00

412.50 (F)

Task 1.4

Use the information from tasks 1.2 and 1.3 to prepare a report. Your report should suggest ONE possible reason for the following variances.

(a) The price variance for white cloth
(b) The usage variance for white cloth
(c) The usage variance for red dye
(d) The labour rate variance
(e) The labour efficiency variance

REPORT

To: **Finance Director** **From: Accounting technician**
Subject: **Date:**

This page is for the continuation of the report.

Additional data

In the financial accounts, stock is valued on an actual cost basis using the FIFO method.

Task 1.5

Use the data given in task 1.1 to calculate the FIFO value of the stock of white cloth at 30 November 2001.

....

....

....

....

....

....

SECTION 2

You should spend about 90 minutes on this section.

Additional data

Design Ltd's operations are organised by departments, as follows:

- Warehouse
- Manufacturing
- Sales
- Administration

The **actual** fixed overheads of the company for November 2001 were as follows.

	£
Depreciation	14,600
Rent	48,000
Other property overheads	12,800
Administration overheads	28,800
Staff costs:	
Warehouse	4,800
Indirect manufacturing	14,340
Sales	12,250
Administration	8,410
Total actual fixed overheads	144,000

The following information is also relevant.

Department	**% of floor space occupied**	**Net book value of fixed assets**
		£'000
Warehouse	20%	160
Manufacturing	65%	560
Sales	5%	40
Administration	10%	40
	100%	800

Overheads are allocated and apportioned between departments using the most appropriate basis.

Task 2.1

Complete the following table showing the allocation and apportionment of actual fixed overheads between the four departments.

Actual fixed overheads for November 2001	Basis	Total £	Warehouse £	Manufacturing £	Sales £	Administration £
Depreciation		14,600				
Rent		48,000				
Other property overheads		12,800				
Administration overheads		28,800				
Staff costs		39,800				
		144,000				

Task 2.2

The table below shows the budgeted fixed overheads for the manufacturing department for November 2001.

Use the information from task 2.1 to complete the table below for the manufacturing department for November 2001.

You should:

(a) identify the actual fixed overheads for each expense
(b) calculate the fixed overhead expenditure variance.

Manufacturing department for November 2001	Actual fixed overheads	Budgeted fixed overheads	Variance
	£	£	£
Depreciation		9,820	
Rent		31,200	
Other property overheads		3,800	
Staff costs		13,305	
Total		58,125	

Additional data

The following data relates to the manufacturing department for November 2001.

	Number of hours
Budgeted direct labour hours	4,650
Actual direct labour hours worked	4,780
Standard direct labour hours produced	4,100

Fixed overheads are absorbed using budgeted direct labour hours.

Task 2.3

This task consists of parts (a) to (d)

Calculate for the manufacturing department for November 2001:

(a) the budgeted fixed overhead absorption rate;

....

....

....

(b) the overhead volume variance;

....

....

....

(c) the overhead efficiency variance;

....

....

....

(d) the overhead capacity variance.

....

....

....

Additional data

The stock of finished goods is valued at standard absorption cost.

Task 2.4

This task consists of parts (a) and (b).

(a) Use the information from tasks 2.2 and 2.3 to prepare the journal entry for the absorption of manufacturing department overheads for November 2001.

Journal	Dr £	Cr £
Finished goods stock		
Overhead expenditure variance		
Overhead volume variance		
Overhead control – manufacturing		

(b) At the end of each month, the finance director of Design Limited prepares a profit and loss account using standard costing.

Explain how the following variances will be recorded in the profit and loss account for November 2001:

(i) the fixed overhead expenditure variance;

....

....

....

....

....

....

....

....

....

(ii) the fixed overhead volume variance.

....

....

....

....

....

....

....

....

....

Task 2.5

(a) Complete the cost report shown below.

(b) Briefly suggest ONE reason for the following variances:

(i) the fixed overhead expenditure variance;
(ii) the fixed overhead capacity variance;
(iii) the fixed overhead efficiency variance.

STANDARD INDIRECT COST REPORT

Department:

Period:

Description	**Favourable variance** £	**Adverse variance** £
Fixed overhead expenditure variance		
Fixed overhead volume variance		
Fixed overhead capacity variance		
Fixed overhead efficiency variance		

COMMENTS

....

....

....

....

....

....

....

....

....

....

....

....

....

This page is for the continuation of the report.

Additional data

The directors of Design Ltd will soon be meeting to agree prices for next year. The finance director asks you to help calculate the cost of the *Rosy Glow* fabric. He gives you the following information.

Monthly manufacturing fixed costs related to Rosy Glow production

	£
Depreciation	1,000
Rent	3,200
Other property overheads	400
Indirect staff costs	1,400
Total	6,000

Unit variable costs per 100 metres of production

	£
White cloth	220.20
Red dye	80.00
Direct labour	30.00

The finance director tells you that the production volume in January will be either:

- 5,000 metres; or
- 6,000 metres.

Task 2.6

Complete the table below to calculate the following for both possible production volumes:

(a) the total cost of production;
(b) the cost per 100 metres.

Product: Rosy glow	**Production**	
Production volume	5,000 metres £	6,000 metres £
Depreciation		
Rent		
Other property overheads		
Indirect staff costs		
White cloth		
Red dye		
Direct labour		
Total cost		
Cost per 100 metres		

Answers to practice activities

CHAPTER 1: COST INFORMATION

1 MIXED FARM

(a) Possible cost units would include a kilogram of crops (such as wheat or barley or oats) or an individual cow/calf/bull.

(b) Possible cost centres include an area (such as a field or an acre), a herd of cattle, the dairy, ploughing activities and harvesting activities.

2 INDIRECT MATERIALS

Strictly speaking this is false. Indirect materials costs are called indirect materials costs! Indirect expenses are indirect costs other than materials or labour. In practice, however, terms like 'cost', 'expense' and 'overhead' are used very loosely.

3 ADVANTAGE

By charging as many costs as possible to cost units rather than treating them as overheads, arbitrary overhead apportionment, resulting in a less accurate cost per unit, is avoided.

4 COST UNITS

(a) A building contractor could treat each contract as a cost unit.

(b) An airline could treat each passenger mile (or 100 or 1,000 passenger miles) as a cost unit.

CHAPTER 2: MATERIALS

5 REORDER LEVELS

The reorder level is influenced by rate of usage and lead time (delivery time).

6 STOCK LEVELS

Minimum stock levels are established for each type of material in a stock control system to allow for unexpected rises in demand and for severe shortages of supply.

7 REQUISITION

(a) A **materials requisition** is used to request and authorise an issue of stock from stores to production.

(b) A **purchase requisition** is used to instruct and authorise the purchasing department to obtain supplies.

8 ANNUAL DEMAND

Economic order quantity (EOQ) = $\sqrt{\frac{2cd}{h}}$, where

c = cost of ordering = £18
d = annual demand = 200,000
h = cost of carrying one unit in stock for one year = £3.20

$$\therefore \text{EOQ} = \sqrt{\frac{2 \times 18 \times 200{,}000}{3.20}} = 1{,}500 \text{ units}$$

9 FIFO TO LIFO

(a) Changing from FIFO to LIFO during a period of rapidly rising prices would result in lower stock valuations.

(b) Changing from FIFO to LIFO during a period of rapidly rising prices would result in higher costs of materials charged to production.

10 OPTIMUM LEVEL

When deciding the optimum level of stock of component parts to be held in a stores serving a mass production assembly line, the following factors should be considered.

(a) The economic order quantity
(b) Deterioration/obsolescence
(c) Space taken up by stores
(d) Cost of capital tied up in stocks
(e) Continuity of supplies

11 MAXIMUM LEVEL

The maximum stock level depends on the reorder level, the reorder quantity, the rate of usage and the delivery time.

CHAPTER 3: LABOUR

12 DIFFERENTIAL PIECEWORK

Piecework is an incentive scheme in that the more output you produce the more you are paid. Differential piecework pays a different rate for different levels of production, for example as follows.

Up to 100 units a day	20p per unit
101 to 150 units a day	22p per unit
151 to 200 units a day	25p per unit
Over 200 units a day	30p per unit

13 EMPLOYEES

Two advantages of paying employees by the results achieved are as follows.

(a) Output should be higher.

(b) Employees can receive higher wages.

14 HOURLY RATES

The majority of employees are paid on the basis of time rather than by results achieved since it can be difficult to measure work done and because quality can suffer if employees try to rush production.

15 WEEKEND WORKING

Additional payments to production workers for weekend working would be treated as a production overhead and not a direct cost since it would be unfair if an item made during overtime hours was more costly just because, by chance, it was made during hours in which employees do not normally work.

The only situation where the additional payments would be treated as a direct cost would be when the weekend working was carried out at the specific request of a customer. In this case, the additional payments would be charged as a direct cost to the customer's order.

CHAPTER 4: EXPENSES

16 PERSONAL COMPUTER

(a) Depreciable amount = £(3,000 – 200) = £2,800.

Expected life = 4 years.

Annual depreciation charge = £2,800/4 = £700.

(b)

	£
Depreciation charged = 3 × £700	2,100
Amount which should have been charged	3,000
Obsolescence charge	900

It is normal practice to charge a loss resulting from obsolescence to the costing profit and loss account.

CHAPTER 5: OVERHEADS AND ABSORPTION COSTING

17 OVERHEAD COSTS

Significant overhead costs incurred by an international firm of management consultants could include the following.

(a) Rent
(b) Travelling expenses
(c) Support staff (secretaries and so on)
(d) Publicity/advertising
(e) Entertaining
(f) Depreciation of computers, wordprocessors and so on

18 ACTUAL OVERHEADS

We need to calculate an overhead absorption rate.

$$\text{Absorption rate} = \frac{\text{budgeted overheads}}{\text{budgeted activity level}} = \frac{£5{,}995}{550 \text{ hrs}}$$

$$= £10.90 \text{ per machine hour}$$

	£
Actual overheads	6,500
Absorbed overheads (540 hrs × £10.90)	5,886
Under-absorbed overheads	614

Under-absorbed overheads reduce the profit for the period.

19 COST DRIVERS

(a) With activity based costing, cost drivers are a means of establishing the overhead cost of activities.

(b) A suitable cost driver for the purchasing department of a large manufacturing company would be the number of purchase orders handled in the period.

20 MACHINING DEPARTMENT

False.

	£
Overheads incurred	9,322
Overheads absorbed (£5 × 1,753)	8,765
Under-absorbed overhead	557

21 MACHINE HOUR RATE METHOD

The overhead absorption rate is calculated by dividing the budgeted/estimated overheads which have been apportioned to the particular production cost centre by the budgeted/estimated number of hours that machines in that production cost centre will be running. Each unit of output is therefore charged with overhead on the basis of the number of machine hours it requires in that cost centre. The machine hour basis should be used if production is highly mechanised such that a large proportion of overhead expenditure is likely to be more closely related to machine utilisation than to direct labour input.

22 ABC

Activity based costing, an alternative to traditional absorption costing, attempts to absorb overheads into product costs on a more realistic basis than that used by traditional absorption costing. The basic idea is that instead of arbitrarily choosing an absorption base for all overheads, overhead costs are grouped according to what drives them or causes them to be incurred. These costs drivers are then used as an absorption basis.

For example, costs associated with handling orders may be driven by the number of orders. The cost driver for such costs is therefore the number of orders. Costs relating to production run set-ups may be driven by the number of set-ups, costs associated with machine activity are driven by the number of machine hours and costs related to labour activity are driven by the number of labour hours.

23 LABOUR INTENSIVE

When using absorption costing, a time-based overhead absorption rate is generally favoured over any other because of the belief that most items of overhead expenditure tend to increase with time. A direct wages percentage rate is to an extent time based, but if differential wage rates exist, this can lead to inequitable overhead absorption. The direct labour hour rate does not suffer from this disadvantage.

Note that ABC is based on the idea that most items of overhead expenditure do not increase with time.

CHAPTER 6: COST BEHAVIOUR

24 COST BEHAVIOUR PATTERNS

Graph of variable cost

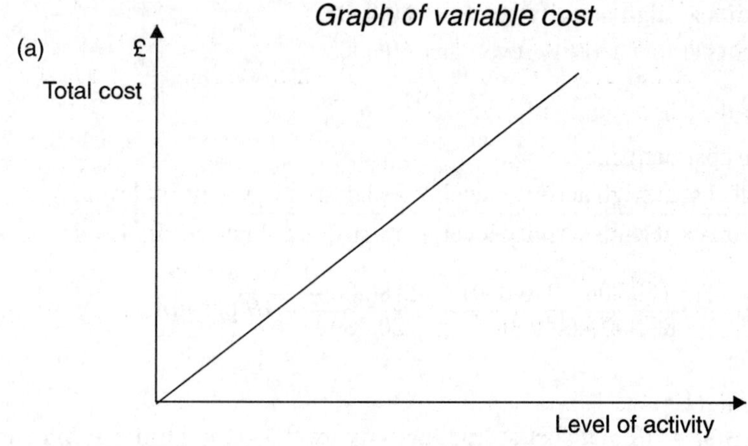

Graph of fixed cost

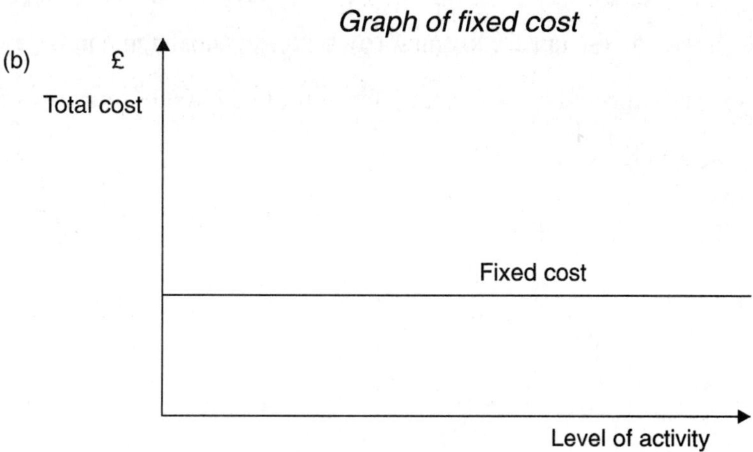

Graph of step cost

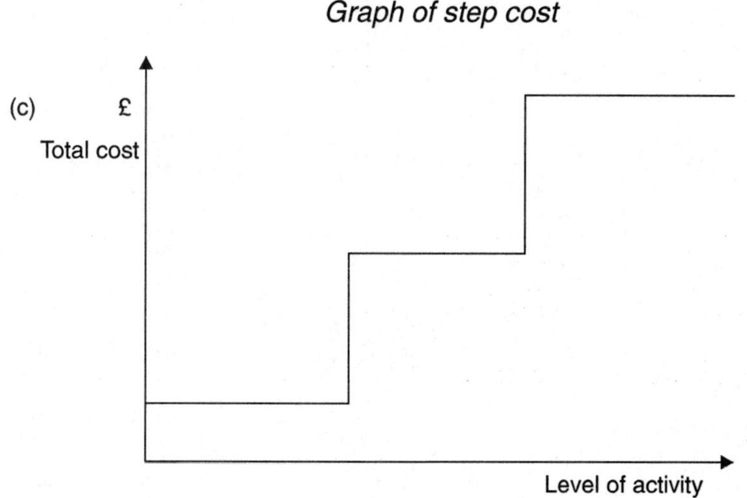

25 LAKE GARDA LTD

Step 1

Period with highest activity = year 2
Period with lowest activity = year 4

Step 2

Total cost at high activity level = £1,150,000
Total cost at low activity level = £970,000
Total units at high activity level = 80,000
Total units at low activity level = 60,000

Step 3

Variable cost per unit =

$$\frac{\text{Total cost at high activity level} - \text{total cost at low activity level}}{\text{Total units at high activity level} - \text{total units at low activity level}}$$

$$= \frac{£(1{,}150{,}000 - 970{,}000)}{80{,}000 - 60{,}000} = \frac{£180{,}000}{20{,}000} = £9 \text{ per unit}$$

Step 4

Fixed costs = (Total cost at high activity level) – (total units at high activity level × variable cost per unit)

= £1,150,000 – (80,000 × £9) = £1,150,000 – 720,000 = £430,000

Therefore, the expected costs in year 5 for output of 75,000 units are as follows.

	£
Variable costs (75,000 × £9)	675,000
Fixed costs	430,000
Total costs	1,105,000

CHAPTER 7: BOOKKEEPING ENTRIES FOR COST INFORMATION

26 FRATERNITY LTD

(a) RAW MATERIALS STOCK

	£		£
Opening balance	34,400	Work in progress (bal figure)	25,640
Creditors (W1)	21,560	Balance c/d	30,320
	55,960		55,960
Balance b/d	15,160		

(b) WORK IN PROGRESS

	£		£
Opening balance	11,200	Finished goods (bal figure)	50,380
Raw materials stock	25,640	Balance c/d	9,500
Direct wages	12,800		
Production overhead (W2)	10,240		
	59,880		59,880
Balance b/d	4,750		

(c) FINISHED GOODS STOCK

	£		£
Opening balance	21,000	P&L account (Cost of sales)	47,200
Work in progress	50,380	Balance c/d	24,180
	71,380		71,380
Balance b/d	12,090		

(d) PRODUCTION OVERHEAD

	£		£
Cash	10,400	Work in progress (W2)	10,240
Depreciation	400	P&L account (under-absorbed)	560
	10,800		10,800

Workings

1 CREDITORS FOR RAW MATERIALS

	£		£
Cash	17,920	Opening balance	15,200
Balance c/f	18,840	Raw materials purchases (bal fig)	21,560
	36,760		36,760

2 Direct labour £12,800
Production overhead absorbed (80%) £10,240

CHAPTER 8: COSTING METHODS

27 BATCH COSTING

Batch costing is a form of costing that is similar to **job costing**, except that costs are collected for a **batch of items**. The cost unit is the **batch**. A cost per unit is calculated by **dividing the total batch cost by the number of units in the batch.**

28 COSTING METHODS

(a) Job costing
(b) Batch costing
(c) Job costing

CHAPTER 9: STANDARD COSTING

29 STANDARD TIME

	Minutes	
A	$200 \times 4 =$	800
B	$350 \times 2 =$	700
C	$300 \times 3 =$	900
		2,400

Standard hours produced = 2,400 ÷ 60 = 40 standard hours.

30 STANDARD COST

It is true that a standard cost is a 'guess' although it may be a very accurate one determined in a highly scientific manner. It is *not* true that standard costs are not relevant once actual costs are known. Standard costs are used not only for planning in advance, but also for monitoring actual performance and deciding whether changes need to be made.

31 IDEAL STANDARD

Advantage Variances from ideal standards are useful for pinpointing areas where a close examination may result in large savings.

Disadvantage They are likely to have an unfavourable motivational impact. Employees will often feel that the goals are unattainable and not work so hard.

CHAPTER 10: CALCULATION OF VARIANCES

32 CASIOS LTD

The workforce of Casios Ltd have been working at a less efficient rate than standard to produce a given output. The result is an **adverse** fixed overhead **efficiency variance.**

The total number of hours worked was, however, more than originally budgeted. The effect is measured by a **favourable** fixed overhead **capacity** variance.

33 VARIANCE

Usage and efficiency variances are quantity variances. They measure the difference between the actual physical quantity of materials used or hours taken and the quantities that should have been used or taken for the actual volume of production. The physical differences are then converted into money values by applying the appropriate standard rate.

34 BRYAN LIMITED

The company spent £500 more on fixed production overheads than budgeted, which is probably not very significant. Units were produced in an average of 2.25 hours each which is a good deal faster than standard. The company also managed to operate for 100 hours longer than expected, and produced 100 extra units. Apart from the slight overspending and assuming the extra units can be sold, all of this is good.

If you calculated the variances you should have got the following figures.

	£
Expenditure	500 (A)
Efficiency	1,200 (F)
Capacity	800 (F)
Total	1,500 (F)

35 RESPONSIBILITY

(a) The production manager

(b) The production manager

CHAPTER 11: FURTHER ASPECTS OF VARIANCE ANALYSIS

36 BEST METHOD

It is usually regarded as better to calculate the materials price variance at the time of receipt of stock, so that it can be eliminated and stocks can be valued at standard price. The advantages are that this reduces clerical work in issuing stocks and variances are highlighted at an earlier stage for management attention. All issues are valued at standard, and it is not necessary to calculate a variance as each issue is made.

37 EXCELSIOR PLC

(a) The variance account affected would be the overhead capacity variance account.

(b) Unit costs of production would increase because the fixed costs would have to be spread over a smaller number of units and therefore each unit would have to bear a larger share of the production overhead.

38 INTERDEPENDENCE

This is term used to express the way in which the cause of one variance may be wholly or partly explained by the cause of another variance. For instance, if the purchasing department buys a cheaper material which is poorer in quality than the expected standard, the material price variance will be favourable, but there may be material wastage and an adverse usage variance.

39 JEMIMA LTD

The cost accounting entry is as follows.

DR Material price variance account
CR Stores ledger control account

GENERAL ACTIVITIES

40 ANALYSIS

	Total	Prime cost	Production expense	Admin. expense	Selling and distribution expense
	£	£	£	£	£
Wages of assembly employees	6,750	6,750			
Wages of stores employees	3,250		3,250		
Tyres for toy wheels	1,420	1,420			
Safety goggles for operators	810		810		
Job advert for new employees	84			84	
Depreciation of delivery vehicles	125				125
Depreciation of production machines	264		264		
Cost of trade exhibition	1,200				1,200
Computer stationery	130			130	
Course fee for AAT training	295			295	
Royalty for the design of wheel 1477	240	240			
	14,568	8,410	4,324	509	1,325

41 PURCHASE INVOICES

(a) (i) and (ii)

Invoice number 3275 Your order number 57623

Date 1.11.X8

	£
50 coils @ £132	6,600
Standard cost of actual quantity (50 × £120)	6,000
Material price variance	600 (A)

Invoice number 4517 Your order number 58127

Date 17.11.X8

	£
150 coils @ £108	16,200
Standard cost of actual quantity (150 × £120)	18,000
Material price variance	1,800 (F)

Invoice number 5178 Your order number 60173

Date 27.11.X8

	£
100 coils @ £120	12,000
Standard cost of actual quantity (100 × £120)	12,000
Material price variance	– (-)

(b) VARIANCE ACCOUNT

1.11.X8	Purchase	600	00	17.11.X8	Purchase	1,800	00

(c) The adverse variance may have been due to careless purchasing by the purchasing department or an unexpected price increase or the loss of a quantity discount because a smaller quantity than standard was purchased. The favourable variance may be due to greater care taken in purchasing by the purchasing department, an unexpected price decrease or an increased quantity discount because a larger quantity than standard was purchased. (The fact that there is no variance when 100 coils are purchased and that there is an adverse variance when less are purchased and a favourable variance when more are purchased suggests that the standard purchase quantity is 100 coils and that the variances are the result of changes to quantity discounts.)

To avoid adverse variances, the purchasing manager should ensure that the cheapest price for material is obtained (although quality of material should not be jeopardised). Material should, if at all possible, be purchased in quantities that ensure the standard discount is received, although care must be taken to ensure that the costs of holding stock are not greater than any quantity discounts received. The responsibility for this lies with the purchasing manager and the stores manager.

42 PROTECTIVE GLOVES

Closing stock = 150 pairs × £1.90 (purchase price on 7.11.X8)
= £285

43 STORES RECORD CARD

Stores Record Card

Material: Paper *Code:* 1564A

		Receipts		*Issues*			*Stock*		
Date	*Details*	*Sheets*	£	*Sheets*	*Price*	£	*Sheets*	*Price*	£
	Opening stock						10,000	0.30	3,000
3 May	Purchase	4,000	1,600				14,000	0.33	4,600
6 May	Issue			7,000	0.33	2,310	7,000	0.33	2,290
12 May	Purchase	10,000	3,100				17,000	0.32	5,390
15 May	Issue			6,000	0.32	1,920	11,000	0.32	3,470
22 May	Issue			7,200	0.32	2,304	3,800	0.32	1,166
25 May	Purchase	10,000	3,200				13,800	0.32	4,366

44 PAPER

Holding large quantities of paper in stock could cause the following problems.

(a) Larger stocks require more storage space and possibly extra staff and equipment to control and handle them.

(b) When material becomes out-of-date and is no longer required, existing stocks must be thrown away and written off to the profit and loss account.

45 OVERHEAD ANALYSIS SHEET

OVERHEAD ANALYSIS SHEET DATE 17.4.X9

	TOTAL	PRODUCTION			SERVICE	
		Cutting	Sewing	Finishing	Stores	Maintenance
	£	£	£	£	£	£
Overheads	603,000	187,000	232,000	106,000	28,000	50,000
Apportion Stores (W1) (a) (Base: Material issued)	-	9,333	11,667	4,667	(28,000)	2,333
Apportion Maintenance (W2) (b) (Base: Machine hours)	-	19,625	32,708	-	-	(52,333)
	603,000	215,958	276,375	110,667		

Workings

1 Total material issued = £'000 (200 + 250 + 100 + 50)
= £600,000

Issued to		*% of total*	*Share of overhead*
			£
Cutting	200/600	$33^1/_3$	9,333
Sewing	250/600	$41^2/_3$	11,667
Finishing	100/600	$16^2/_3$	4,667
Maintenance	50/600	$8^1/_3$	2,333
		100	28,000

2 Total machine hours = 15,000 + 25,000 = 40,000.

Worked in		*% of total*	*Share of overhead*
			£
Cutting	15,000/40,000	$37^1/_2$	19,625
Sewing	25,000/40,000	$62^1/_2$	32,708
			52,333

46 LABOUR HOURS

Department	*Basis of absorption*	*Hours*	*Overhead*	*Overhead absorption rate*
			£	
Cutting	Machine hours	15,000	215,958	£14.40 per machine hour
Sewing	Machine hours	25,000	276,375	£11.06 per machine hour
Finishing	Labour hours	12,000	110,667	£9.22 per labour hour
			603,000	

47 MACHINE HOUR RATES

Machine hour rates should be used in the cutting and sewing departments because activity levels and output depend on the number of machine hours worked in the department. Overhead costs are likely to be related to machine time, for example depreciation and power costs. Therefore a product which utilises more machine time should absorb more production overhead cost.

48 XL

STANDARD PRODUCT COST SHEET
PRODUCT : 'XL'

Date: XX.XX.XX

	Hours	Rate £	£	£
Direct Material Cost				4.32
Direct Labour Cost				
- cutting	¼	8.00	2.00	
- sewing	1	6.00	6.00	
- finishing	½	10.00	5.00	
Total Labour Cost				13.00
Overhead Cost				
- cutting	¼	14.40	3.60	
- sewing	1	11.06	11.06	
- finishing	½	9.22	4.61	
Total Overhead Cost				19.27
TOTAL COST				36.59

49 MATERIAL METRES

(a) (i) **Material price variance**

	£
50 metres should have cost (× £3.00)	150
but did cost (× £2.00)	100
Material price variance	50 (F)

(ii) **Material usage variance**

20 garments should have used (× 2m)	40 m
but did use	50 m
Material usage variance (in metres)	10 m (A)
× standard price per metre	× £3
Material usage variance (in £)	£30 (A)

(iii) **Total material cost variance**

	£
20 garments should have cost (× £3.00 × 2m)	120
but did cost	100
Total material cost variance	20 (F)

(b) Price variance - purchasing manager

Usage variance - production manager

(c) Providing the quality of the material was unaffected, it appears that the material should have been bought because the overall material cost variance was favourable. The adverse variance arising from the use of substandard material was more than compensated for by the favourable price variance arising from the use of cheaper material. However, we have no information concerning labour times. If the cheaper material was difficult to process this could have led to adverse efficiency variances on labour and overhead.

50 TABLE START

To complete this practice activity you have to allocate to the five departments those overheads which are directly associated with the departments.

	Forming	*Colouring*	*Assembly*	*Maintenance*	*General*	*Total*
	£	£	£	£	£	£
Directly allocated overheads:						
Repairs, maintenance	800	1,800	300	200	100	3,200
Departmental expenses	1,500	2,300	1,100	900	1,500	7,300
Indirect labour	3,000	5,000	1,500	4,000	2,000	15,500
	5,300	9,100	2,900	5,100	3,600	26,000

51 TABLE FINISH

This practice activity involves apportioning the remaining overheads (those which have not been directly allocated) to the five departments.

		Forming	*Colouring*	*Assembly*	*Maintenance*	*General*	*Total*
		£	£	£	£	£	£
Directly allocated overheads:							
Repairs, maintenance		800	1,800	300	200	100	3,200
Departmental expenses		1,500	2,300	1,100	900	1,500	7,300
Indirect labour		3,000	5,000	1,500	4,000	2,000	15,500
		5,300	9,100	2,900	5,100	3,600	26,000
Apportionment of other overheads							
Rent, rates	1	1,600	3,200	2,400	400	400	8,000
Power	2	200	450	75	25	0	750
Light, heat	1	1,000	2,000	1,500	250	250	5,000
Dep'n of plant	3	2,500	6,000	750	750	0	10,000
Dep'n of F & F	4	50	25	100	50	25	250
Insurance of plant	3	500	1,200	150	150	0	2,000
Insurance of buildings	1	100	200	150	25	25	500
		11,250	22,175	8,025	6,750	4,300	52,500

Basis of apportionment:

1 floor area
2 effective horsepower
3 plant value
4 fixtures and fittings

52 REPEATED DISTRIBUTION METHOD

To complete this practice activity you had to use the information provided on the number of hours work the two service departments are budgeted to do for the other departments (and each other).

	Forming	*Colouring*	*Assembly*	*Maintenance*	*General*	*Total*
	£	£	£	£	£	£
Allocated and apportioned overheads	11,250	22,175	8,025	6,750	4,300	52,500
Apportion maintenance	1,350	3,375	1,350	(6,750)	675	
					4,975	
Apportion general	995	2,985	498	497	(4,975)	
Apportion maintenance	99	249	99	(497)	50	
Apportion general	10	30	5	5	(50)	
Apportion maintenance	1	3	1	(5)		
	13,705	28,817	9,978			52,500

53 THREE DEPARTMENTS

The forming and assembly departments are labour intensive. We can deduce this from the information on the relative number of labour and machine hours in each department. The overhead absorption rate (OAR) for these two departments should therefore be based on labour hours. The colouring department, on the other hand, is machine intensive. Machine hours should therefore be used as the basis of the overhead absorption rate.

Department			**OAR**
Forming	$\frac{£13,705}{27,400}$	=	£0.50 per labour hour
Colouring	$\frac{£28,817}{14,400}$	=	£2.00 per machine hour
Assembly	$\frac{£9,978}{20,000}$	=	£0.50 per labour hour

54 DECEMBER 20X9

The under-/over-absorbed overhead is calculated as the difference between the overhead actually incurred and the overhead absorbed. The overhead absorbed is the OAR × actual number of the basis of the absorption rate.

	Overhead incurred		*Overhead absorbed*	*(Under)-/over-absorbed overhead*
	£		£	£
Forming	14,580	(30,000 × £0.50)	15,000	420
Colouring	30,050	(16,000 × £2.00)	32,000	1,950
Assembly	9,840	(18,500 × £0.50)	9,250	(590)
Over-absorbed overhead				1,780

55 POLTIMORE PLC

JOB 212/A

	£		£
Balance b/f	11,022	Materials transfer	3,500
Materials	3,122	Cost of sales	16,410
Labour	1,922		
Production overhead (W1)			
(200% of direct wages)	3,844		
	19,910		19,910

JOB 219/C

	£		£
Materials	4,003	Cost of sales	29,268
Materials transfer	3,500		
Labour	7,255		
Production overhead (W1)			
(200% of direct wages)	14,510		
	29,268		29,268

Workings

1 **Job 212/A Costs to date**

	£
Production overhead	2,628
Direct labour	1,314

∴ Production overhead absorption rate $= \frac{£2,628}{£1,314} \times 100\%$ of direct wages

$= 200\%$ of direct wages

56 PROFIT OR LOSS

	212/A	*219/C*
	£	£
Factory cost	16,410	29,268
Administration and marketing overheads	2,462	4,390
Cost of sale	18,872	33,658
Invoice value	20,500	28,750
Profit/(loss)	1,628	(4,908)

Answers to practice devolved assessments

ANSWERS TO PRACTICE DEVOLVED ASSESSMENT 1: STRANGE (PROPERTIES) LTD

Helping hand. Your approach to this assessment is more important than arriving at an answer that agrees with ours to the penny, so don't be disheartened if your figures are a bit different.

Answer

Task 1

(a)

No.	Date	Description	Code	Total
	November			£
1	1	Caretaker - Clerk Court	800/999	76.50
2	1	Sankey Builders, Sheen - Ketley	800/556	600.00
3	1	Post Office	400/001	3.61
4	1	Sundries - Gibbs Ho	800/105	52.80
5	1	Perivale Glass Co.	800/101	317.00
6	3	Motor Mower - Burgess Ct	800/555	263.00
7	4	Electricity - Ketley cl. (to 28.10)	800/556	355.84
8	4	Water rates - Q.C.	800/225	92.00
9	4	Inst. Ch. Surveyors	500/003	515.00
10	5	Hanwell DIY	800/501	69.10
11	8	Law Society (subs)	500/003	742.00
12	8	Inland Revenue	100/003	8,437.50
13	8	Gas - Mallow Cl. (to 5.11)	800/605	81.50
14	9	Cleaners - Seymour M.	800/189	390.01
15	10	Power drill - Laine Ho.	800/501	48.90
16	13	Perivale Roofing	800/101	4,720.00
17	17	Dentons (sols) - re Ashby M.	800/301	723.37
18	17	Coomer PL - Caretaker	800/450	226.00
19	17	Kew Electrics	800/250	590.72
20	17	Southern Electricity (to 15.11)	300/001	1,110.43
21	17	Wyrde St Computer Supplies	400/004	33.00
22	18	Brentford Advertiser	700/001	66.50
23	19	Rentokil - Jones Co.	800/274	856.06
24	21	Neville Ho - Skip Hire (17.10-19.11)	800/376	32.40
25	21	Hanwell Timber	800/501	236.00
26	21	Sankeys - Ketley Clo.	800/556	1,800.00
27	24	Heston Service Station	200/001	8.81
28	24	Bldgs Ins - Oakwood B	800/750	408.00
29	24	Plumbing Supplies (Petersham) Ltd - Kings	800/325	426.80
30	24	Wages - Grasmere Caretaker	800/110	279.19
31	25	BACS - Salaries	100/002	12,187.89
32	25	British Gas - Tilbury	800/890	35.60

No.	Date	Description	Code	Total
	November			
33	26	Hall hire - Wyndham AGM	800/430	32.50
34	26	Sainsbury's	100/010	19.50
35	28	Caretaker - Rodway Ho.	800/001	438.00
36	28	Property Management News	700/001	18.40
37	28	British Telecom	400/002	475.70
38	28	Co. House - Wyndham	800/430	32.00
39	28	Concrete repairs - Tilbury T	800/890	2,250.00
40	28	Acton Skip Hire - 1.11-30.11 - Davison	800/801	32.40
41	28	Brentford Cleaning	300/005	183.00
42	28	Wages - Davison Clo. C/T	800/801	66.10
43	28	Wages - Endymion Pl. C/T	800/675	64.50
44	28	Middlesex Gazette	700/001	22.22
45	28	Ben Smith Stationery Supplies	400/003	178.57
46	28	Electricity - Hennigan Ho. (to 25.11)	800/429	568.35
47	28	Guardian Royal Exchange - Pub. Liab	500/002	970.00
48	28	Guardian Royal Exchange - Richm. Bldgs	800/525	1,630.00
49	28	E Strange Exps	900/001	88.90
50	28	Non-Dom Rates DD	300/003	271.25
51	28	GRE Insurance- Jaguar	200/002	1,315.50
52	28	Bank - charges	600/002	70.90
53	28	Bank - interest	600/001	949.93
54				
55				
56				
57				
58				
59				
60				
61				
62				
63				
64				

(b) **Client charges - November 20X2**

		Direct expenses	*Fixed fee*	*Share of overheads*	*Total*
		£	£	£	£
301	Ashby Mansions	723.37	1,500.00	922.29	3,145.66
555	Burgess Court	263.00	1,500.00	922.29	2,685.29
999	Clerk Court	76.50	1,500.00	922.29	2,498.79
350	Clift Flats	-	1,500.00	922.29	2,422.29
620	Clifton Gardens	-	1,500.00	922.29	2,422.29
450	Coomer Place	226.00	1,500.00	922.29	2,648.29
801	Davison Close	98.50	1,500.00	922.29	2,520.79
261	De Beauvoir Buildings	-	1,500.00	922.29	2,422.29
675	Endymion Place	64.50	1,500.00	922.29	2,486.79
401	Frampton Court	-	1,500.00	922.29	2,422.29
105	Gibbs House	52.80	1,500.00	922.29	2,475.09
101	Glebe Gardens	5,037.00	1,500.00	922.29	7,459.29
110	Grasmere Mansion	279.19	1,500.00	922.29	2,701.48
429	Hennigan House	568.35	1,500.00	922.29	2,990.64
274	Jones Court	856.06	1,500.00	922.29	3,278.35
556	Ketley Close	2,755.84	1,500.00	922.29	5,178.13
325	Kings Buildings	426.80	1,500.00	922.29	2,849.09
501	Laine House	354.00	1,500.00	922.29	2,776.29
250	Loudwater Place	590.72	1,500.00	922.29	3,013.01
100	Matkins Gardens	-	1,500.00	922.29	2,422.29
605	Mallow Close	81.50	1,500.00	922.29	2,503.79
376	Neville House	32.40	1,500.00	922.29	2,454.69
750	Oakwood Buildings	408.00	1,500.00	922.29	2,830.29
225	Queen's Court	92.00	1,500.00	922.29	2,514.29
914	Rhodes Close	-	1,500.00	922.29	2,422.29
001	Rodway House	438.00	1,500.00	922.29	2,860.29
189	Seymour Manor	390.01	1,500.00	922.29	2,812.30
890	Tilbury Tower	2,285.60	1,500.00	922.29	4,707.89
525	Undercliff Gardens	1,630.00	1,500.00	922.29	4,052.29
430	Wyndham Rise	64.50	1,500.00	922.29	2,486.79
		17,794.64	45,000.00	27,668.70	90,463.34

(*Helping hand.* You should calculate to the penny because clients are invoiced in pounds and pence.)

Task 2

Basis	*Legal*	*Surveying*	*Accounts*	*Total*
	£	£	£	£
Employees (W1)	91,264	127,770	54,759	273,793
Floor area (W2)	5,367	10,735	5,367	21,469
Directors (W3)	4,316	4,315	-	8,631
Equal split (W4)	10,313	10,313	10,313	30,939
	111,260	153,133	70,439	334,832

Workings

1 The following expenses should be split on the basis of number of employees.

	£
Wages and salaries	272,255
Staff welfare	1,538
	273,793

	Legal	*Surveying*	*Accounts*
Split 5:7:3	£91,264	£127,770	£54,759

(*Helping hand.* The split should really be done on the basis of the actual payroll analysis. The above is likely to be a reasonable approximation however.)

2 The following expenses can be split on the basis of floor area, which can be seen (by simply looking at the floor plan) to be 1:2:1.

	£
Business rates	3,524
Heat and light	4,775
Buildings depreciation	4,000
Office equipment depreciation	1,752
Repairs and maintenance	834
Cleaning	6,584
	21,469

	Legal	*Surveying*	*Accounts*
1:2:1	£5,367	£10,735	£5,367

3 Some of the expenses are incurred solely by the two Strange brothers.

	£
Motor vehicle depreciation	7,500
Subscriptions	1,131
	8,631

These are split 50:50 between the legal and surveying departments.

4 The remaining expenses do not have any obvious basis and it is therefore most appropriate to split these equally between the three departments.

	£
Insurance (see note)	7,600
Telecommunications	1,908
Printing, postage and stationery	3,975
Audit and accountancy	4,500
Bank charges	862
Advertising	1,973
Interest	10,121
	30,939

(*Helping hand.* It would be better to split the insurance figure between buildings, motor vehicles, public liability, employer's liability and so on, and then apportion it on more appropriate bases, but you have not been given enough information to do this.)

You can now calculate a rate per labour hour, as it were, for the absorption of overheads.

Legal department

$$\frac{£111{,}260}{1{,}709} = £65.10 \text{ per hour (say £65)}$$

(Note that the overhead is to be absorbed by hours spent on existing clients only.)

Surveying department

$$\frac{£153{,}133}{1{,}749} = £87.55 \text{ per hour (say £88)}$$

Accounts department

Evenly divided between over 30 clients:

$$\frac{£70{,}439}{30} = £2{,}347.97 \text{ per client per annum (say £2,348)}$$

This allows a schedule to be drawn up as follows.

	Legal		*Surveying*		*Accounts*	*Total*
	Hours	£	Hours	£	£	£
Ashby Mansions	43	2,795	20	1,760	2,348	6,903
Burgess Court	71	4,615	82	7,216	2,348	14,179
Clerk Court	62	4,030	34	2,992	2,348	9,370
Clift Flats	15	975	113	9,944	2,348	13,267
Clifton Gardens	25	1,625	64	5,632	2,348	9,605
Coomer Place	60	3,900	80	7,040	2,348	13,288
Davison Close	49	3,185	52	4,576	2,348	10,109
De Beauvoir Buildings	74	4,810	38	3,344	2,348	10,502
Endymion Place	33	2,145	51	4,488	2,348	8,981
Frampton Court	16	1,040	73	6,424	2,348	9,812
Gibbs House	51	3,315	21	1,848	2,348	7,511
Glebe Gardens	81	5,265	60	5,280	2,348	12,893
Grasmere Mansion	84	5,460	30	2,640	2,348	10,448
Hennigan House	76	4,940	94	8,272	2,348	15,560
Jones Court	61	3,965	66	5,808	2,348	12,121
Ketley Close	49	3,185	36	3,168	2,348	8,701
Kings Buildings	63	4,095	57	5,016	2,348	11,459
Laine House	45	2,925	77	6,776	2,348	12,049
Loudwater Place	73	4,745	48	4,224	2,348	11,317
Matkins Gardens	76	4,940	35	3,080	2,348	10,368
Mallow Close	57	3,705	61	5,368	2,348	11,421
Neville House	24	1,560	92	8,096	2,348	12,004
Oakwood Buildings	117	7,605	40	3,520	2,348	13,473
Queen's Court	51	3,315	18	1,584	2,348	7,247
Rhodes Close	82	5,330	97	8,536	2,348	16,214
Rodway House	64	4,160	88	7,744	2,348	14,252
Seymour Manor	23	1,495	64	5,632	2,348	9,475
Tilbury Tower	29	1,885	59	5,192	2,348	9,425
Undercliff Gardens	80	5,200	71	6,248	2,348	13,796
Wyndham Rise	75	4,875	28	2,464	2,348	9,687
	1,709	111,085	1,749	153,912	70,440	335,437
Total overhead		111,260		153,133	70,439	334,832
(Under-)/over-absorbed		(175)		779	1	605

Notes

1 The (under)/over absorption is due to rounding, for ease of calculation.

2 The amount that **actually** was charged to each client for the year to 30 September, in respect of a share of the overheads, can be estimated as follows, allowing for ex-clients.

$$\frac{\text{(Administrative expenses + interest)}}{\text{Number of clients}}$$

$$= \frac{£(324{,}711+10{,}121)}{32.5(\text{say})}$$

$$= £10{,}303$$

Task 3

MEMO

To: Edward Strange
From: John Vernon
Subject: Charges to clients and related matters
Date: 2 December 20X2

CHARGES TO CLIENTS

I refer to your memo of 1 December about charges to clients. I have given this matter some thought and done some calculations. The results are attached. Below I set out my observations and recommendations.

(a) Part of the problem is due to the way in which we invoice clients. At present our invoices show only a lump sum charge, whereas in fact the charge is made up of three elements, as follows.

 (i) Expenditure incurred on behalf of the property in question on things like building work, bills for communal electricity, caretaker's wages and so on. The property would have to pay these amounts whether or not we were involved, and they are bound to fluctuate from month to month, just as ordinary household expenses do. For example, for the month just past such expenses range from nil for six clients to £5,037 for Glebe Gardens.

 (ii) Our fixed fee of £1,500 per month charged to all clients.

 (iii) A proportion of our own expenses, divided up equally between clients (see below).

(b) Point (iii) above is problematic because our own actual expenditure varies from month to month and so, therefore, does the amount charged to clients. For example in November 20X2 we paid a number of bills that we receive on a quarterly basis (like telephone and electricity bills) and some that only occur annually (like your motor insurance premium). However, all of this expenditure will be charged to our clients in one month.

(c) You may remember that I mentioned to you that I had had some less than complimentary letters from some clients and ex-clients about the fairness of our charges. At present clients for whom we do relatively little work pay the same level of charges as clients for whom we do a great deal of work, and some of them seem to be aware of this and to resent it.

My recommendations are as follows.

(a) We should show the following separately on our invoices.

 (i) Amounts paid out on behalf of clients
 (ii) The charge made for our services (the amount on which VAT is calculated)

(b) Developing (ii), we should charge our clients a standard monthly amount that incorporates the following.

 (i) Our fixed fee

 (ii) An administration charge based on the amount of work that we expect to do for each client

The calculation of the administration charge will require us to estimate in advance both how much our total administrative expenses will be for the coming year and how much work we expect to do for each client. Pending further discussion, however, I have calculated some figures based on the accounts for the year to 30 September 20X2 and upon your own timesheets for that period and those of your brother.

From the 20X1/X2 accounts we can work out that the amount actually charged to each client to recover administrative expenses and interest paid was about £10,303 for the year. Using the fairer basis that I propose this figure would have ranged from £6,903 for Ashby Mansions to £16,214 for Rhodes Close (neither of these figures includes the fixed fee).

I propose that we adopt the fairer basis, assuming that our costs and expenditure in terms of time can be reasonably accurately forecast. Obviously we need to consider how this change would be presented to clients.

OTHER MATTERS

Since you raised the question I might add that what I am proposing is a form of absorption costing: our costs are being 'absorbed' into the amounts charged to clients on the basis of time spent. A feature of absorption costing is 'under- or over-absorbed overhead', which arises because we use estimates to calculate our absorption rates and an adjustment has to be made once the actual figures are known. For example on the schedules attached you can see the effects of rounding some of the figures to make the calculations easier to do and to understand.

Incidentally, I think you may have been misled about the nature of *process costing*. This is a method of costing that is used mainly in manufacturing businesses where products are made by means of a 'continuous process'. In other words there are always some products that have just been started, some that are completely finished and others that are only partly finished. An organisation like this has to use process costing methods to determine the cost of their products at a particular point in time. This is not really appropriate for Strange (Properties) Ltd's business.

ANSWERS TO PRACTICE DEVOLVED ASSESSMENT 2: STATELY HOTELS PLC

SECTION 1

Task 1

		£
(a)	8,580 soap packs should have cost (× £1.20)	10,296
	but did cost (W1)	10,614
	Soap pack price variance	318 (A)
(b)	8,400 rooms should have used	8,400 packs
	but did use	8,580 packs
	Usage variance in packs	180 packs (A)
	× standard price per pack	× £1.20
	Soap pack usage variance	£216 (A)
		£
(c)	2,550 hours should have cost (× £7.20)	18,360
	but did cost (W2)	17,400
	Cleaning labour rate variance	960 (F)
(d)	8,400 rooms should have taken (× ¼ hr)	2,100 hrs
	but did take	2,550 hrs
	Efficiency variance in hours	450 hrs (A)
	× standard rate per hour	× £7.20
	Cleaning labour efficiency variance	£3,240 (A)

Workings

1		£
	6,530 × £1.20	7,836
	920 × £1.30	1,196
	1,130 × £1.40	1,582
		10,614
		£
2	1,850 × £6.00	11,100
	700 × £9	6,300
		17,400

Task 2

The **adverse price variance** could be due to an increase in soap pack prices above the price used in the standard or careless purchasing by the purchasing department.

The **adverse usage variance** may be due to a delivery of low quality soap packs (perhaps packs have items missing or the packaging is ripped) or there may be theft or pilferage of the packs from stores.

The **favourable rate variance** has probably arisen because the proportion of weekday hours worked was greater than anticipated.

The **adverse efficiency variance** may be due to a level of idle time greater than that allowed for in the standard, perhaps because guests had not vacated rooms and cleaners were unable to enter bedrooms.

SECTION 2

Task 1

(a)

	£
26,500 kg should have cost (× £23)	609,500
but did cost	662,500
Material price variance	53,000 (A)

(b)

9,000 units should have used (×3 kg)	27,000 kg
but did use	26,500 kg
Material usage variance in kg	500 kg (F)
× standard price per kg	£23
Material usage variance	£11,500 (F)

(c)

	£
18,400 hours should have cost (× £20)	368,000
but did cost	349,600
Labour rate variance	18,400 (F)

(d)

9,000 units should have taken (× 2 hrs)	18,000 hrs
but did take	18,400 hrs
Efficiency variance in hours	400 hrs (A)
× standard rate per hour	£20
Labour efficiency variance in £	£8,000 (A)

Task 2

STATEMENT OF COST VARIANCES (WEEK 8, QUARTER 4, 20X0)

	(F)	(A)		
	£	£	£	
Material price		53,000		
Material usage	11,500			
Labour rate	18,400			
Labour efficiency		8,000		
Fixed overhead expenditure		300,000		
Fixed overhead capacity		96,000		
Fixed overhead efficiency		24,000		
	29,900	481,000	451,100	(A)

SECTION 3

Task 1

(a)

	£
Budgeted fixed overhead expenditure (12,000 × £67)	804,000
Actual fixed overhead expenditure	824,000
Fixed overhead expenditure variance	20,000 (A)

(b)

	£
Budgeted production at standard rate (12,000 × £67)	804,000
Actual production at standard rate (11,200 × £67)	750,400
Fixed overhead volume variance	53,600 (A)

(c)

Budgeted hours (12,000 × 10)	120,000 hrs
Actual hours	110,000 hrs
Fixed overhead capacity variance in hours	10,000 hrs (A)
× standard rate per hour	× £6.70
Fixed overhead capacity variance	£67,000 (A)

(d)

11,200 units should have taken (× 10 hrs)	112,000 hrs
Actual time taken	110,000 hrs
Fixed overhead efficiency variance in hours	2,000 hrs (F)
× standard rate per hour	× £6.70
Fixed overhead efficiency variance	£13,400 (F)

Task 2

REPORT

To: Production Director
From: Assistant Management Accountant
Date: 14 December 20X0
Subject: Performance of Division X - four weeks ended 1 December 20X0

Set out below is an analysis of the cost variances in Division X for the four-week period ended 1 December 20X0.

Variances	(F)	(A)	
	£	£	£
Material price		94,000	
Material usage		88,000	
Labour rate		11,000	
Labour efficiency	16,800		
Fixed overhead expenditure		20,000	
Fixed overhead capacity		67,000	
Fixed overhead efficiency	13,400		
	30,200	280,000	249,800 (A)

Task 3

MEMORANDUM

To: Production director
From: Assistant management accountant
Date: 14 December 20X0
Subject: Fixed overhead variances

This memorandum provides information on fixed overhead variances. In particular it covers the meaning of the various fixed overhead variances and the ways in which such variances might arise.

The meaning of fixed overhead variances

Whereas labour and material total variances show the effect on costs and hence profit of the difference between what the actual production volume should have cost and what it did cost (in terms of labour or material), if an organisation uses standard absorption costing (as we do), the fixed overhead total variance is the difference between actual fixed overhead expenditure and the fixed overhead absorbed (the under- or over-absorbed overhead).

The total under or over absorption is made up of the fixed overhead expenditure variance and the fixed overhead volume variance. The volume variance shows that part of the under- or over-absorbed overhead which is due to any difference between budgeted production volume and actual production volume.

The volume variance can be further broken down into an efficiency variance and a capacity variance. The capacity variance shows how much of the under- or over-absorbed overhead is due to working the labour force or plant less or more than planned whereas the efficiency variance shows the effect of the efficiency of the labour force or plant.

The volume variance and its two subdivisions, the efficiency variance and the capacity variance, measure the extent of under or over absorption due to production volume being different to that planned. Material usage and labour efficiency variances, on the other hand, measure the effect of usage being different from that expected for the actual volume achieved.

The expenditure variance indicates the amount of under- or over-absorbed overhead which is due to any difference between budgeted fixed overhead expenditure and actual fixed overhead expenditure.

Reasons why fixed overhead variances might arise

Under- or over-absorbed fixed overhead is inevitable because the predetermined overhead absorption rates are based on forecasts about expenditure and the level of activity. These forecasts are always likely to be at least a bit inaccurate - the business may forecast both the budgeted expenditure and the volume of activity wrongly.

- A fixed overhead expenditure variance arises when the actual fixed production overhead is different to the budgeted figure. In our case the actual fixed overhead expenditure was £20,000 more than was forecast for the four weeks ended 1 December. This could have arisen, for example, if rent had been increased and this had not been taken into account when preparing the forecast.

- The fixed overhead volume variance is broken down into efficiency and capacity variances, which have arisen as follows:

  The staff worked at a more efficient rate than standard to produce the 11,200 Alphas that were made in the period. They took 2,000 hours less than would have been expected for that level of production, possibly because of increased speed as newer workers became more accustomed to the processes, or less idle time as a result of fewer mechanical breakdowns. This has led to a favourable efficiency variance.

  Regardless of the level of efficiency and the number of Alphas produced, the overall total number of hours worked was 10,000 less than budgeted. This could arise through a strike, early closing, or some other incident that led to actual hours worked being less than expected. This created an adverse capacity variance, because fixed overhead was under-absorbed as a result.

Answers to trial run devolved assessment

ANSWERS TO TRIAL RUN DEVOLVED ASSESSMENT: FOOD WITH A BITE

DO NOT TURN THIS PAGE UNTIL YOU HAVE COMPLETED THE TRIAL RUN DEVOLVED ASSESSMENT

STANDARD COST CARD

PRODUCT Vegetarian Chilli

DESCRIPTION	QUANTITY	COST PER KG/HOUR/ETC	EXTENSION	TOTAL
Materials		£	£	£
Rice	0.125 kg	1.37	0.17	
Lentils	0.0625 kg	0.88	0.06	
Tomatoes	0.167 kg	0.74	0.12	
Mushrooms etc	0.167 kg	1.22	0.20	
Kidney beans	0.167 kg	0.92	0.15	
Chillis	0.025 kg	1.82	0.05	
Cartons	1	0.05	0.05	
SUB-TOTAL				0.80
Labour				
Production	0.025 hr	4.00	0.10	
SUB-TOTAL				0.10
Direct cost				0.90
Variable o/h	0.01 litre	1.75		0.02
Standard variable cost				0.92
Fixed o/h	0.025 hr	10.11		0.25
Standard cost of sale				1.17

STANDARD COST CARD

PRODUCT Vegetarian Curry

DESCRIPTION	QUANTITY	COST PER KG/HOUR/ETC	EXTENSION	TOTAL
Materials		£	£	£
Rice	0.125 kg	1.37	0.17	
Coconut oil	0.167 litre	1.21	0.20	
Spices	0.005 kg	9.66	0.05	
Vegetables	0.167 kg	1.12	0.19	
Cartons	1	0.05	0.05	
SUB-TOTAL				0.66
Labour				
Production	0.033 hr	4.00	0.13	
SUB-TOTAL				0.13
Direct cost				0.79
Variable o/h	0.01 litre	1.75		0.02
Standard variable cost				0.81
Fixed o/h	0.033 hr	8.45		0.28
Standard cost of sale				1.09

(a) (i) Standard quantities are taken from Delia Craddock's letter.

(ii) The standard price per kilogram, hour and so on are calculated as follows, using the price list and compliment slip from Exotic Foods Emporium.

Item	*Quantity*	*Price at 1.3.X3*	*5%*	*Mid-year value*	*Cost per unit*
		£	£	£	£
Rice	100 kg	130.00	6.50	136.50	1.37
Lentils	100 kg	84.00	4.20	88.20	0.88
Tomatoes	50 kg	35.00	1.75	36.75	0.74
Mushrooms etc	50 kg	58.00	2.90	60.90	1.22
Kidney beans	50 kg	44.00	2.20	46.20	0.92
Chillis	50 kg	86.50	4.33	90.83	1.82
Coconut oil	100 ltrs	115.00	5.75	120.75	1.21
Spices	10 kg	92.00	4.60	96.60	9.66
Vegetables	50 kg	53.50	2.68	56.18	1.12

(iii) Carton price from quotation.

(b) (i) Standard times are taken from the business plan.

(ii) The standard rates per hour are taken from the offers of employment. The business plan recommended that overtime should not be a regular occurrence. Overtime premium should therefore not be included in the direct cost of the two products.

(c) Details of the oil are taken from the telephone message. The current price is used as the standard since the message indicates that the price is unlikely to change in the future.

(d) (i) We need to concern ourselves with the following overheads.

	Annual overhead budget £	
Salary of supervisor	16,000	(from offer of employment)
Salary of storekeeper	12,000	(from offer of employment)
Cleaners (2 hrs × £10 × 5 days × 52 weeks)	5,200	(from contract)
Heat and light	5,000	(from Business Plan)
Overtime premium (100 hrs × £2.00)	200	(from Business Plan)
	38,400	

Although, in reality, there would be many more overheads such as those associated with the accounting function and so on, we calculate an overhead absorption rate based on the limited information we are given.

		Overhead	*Basis of apportionment*	*Production dept Chilli* £	*Production dept Curry* £	*Stores* £
(ii)	Directly allocate	Storekeeper's salary				12,000
(iii)	Apportion	Supervisor's salary	Direct labour hours (W1)	7,500	8,500	-
		Cleaners	Area (W2)	2,600	1,560	1,040
		Heat and light	Area (W2)	2,500	1,500	1,000
		Overtime premium	Hours (W3)	100	100	-
				12,700	11,660	14,040
(iv)	Apportion service dept o'hds		Number of material requi-sitions (W4)	7,020	7,020	(14,040)
				19,720	18,680	-

Workings

		Chilli	*Curry*
1	Budgeted production (portions)	78,000	66,300
	Time per portion	1.5 mins	2 mins
	Budgeted total time	117,000 mins	132,600 mins
		= 1,950 hrs	= 2,210 hrs
	Proportion of salary	1,950/(1,950 + 2,210)	2,210/(1,950 + 2,210)

2 Chilli department covers $25 \times 50 = 1{,}250 \text{ m}^2$

Curry department covers $25 \times 30 = 750 \text{ m}^2$

Stores covers $25 \times 20 = 500 \text{ m}^2$

Cleaning costs and heat and light should therefore be shared in the ratio 5:3:2.

3 We are given no indication as to the amount of overtime each product will require. The overhead should therefore be split equally between the two production departments.

4 Ingredients for both products were taken on each of the five occasions items were taken from stores. One simple method of splitting the stores cost is therefore equally between the two production departments. If Ali and Fred had taken ingredients for just one of the products on one or more occasions then a different apportionment of the overhead would be necessary.

(v) The overhead absorption rate is to be based on direct labour hours according to the business plan. We calculated the budgeted labour hours in each production department in Working 1.

$$\text{Overhead absorption rate - chilli} = \frac{£19{,}720}{1{,}950 \text{ hrs}} = £10.11 \text{ per direct labour hour}$$

$$\text{Overhead absorption rate - curry} = \frac{£18{,}680}{2{,}210 \text{ hrs}} = £8.45 \text{ per direct labour hour}$$

(e)

5,000 portions should take (× 2 mins)	166.67 hrs
But did take (from clock cards) (W1)	170.50 hrs
Efficiency variance, (in hours)	3.83 hrs (A)
× standard rate per hour	× £4
Efficiency variance, (in £)	£15.32 (A)

Working

Calculation of actual hours worked

Week ending	*M* Hours	*T* Hours	*W* Hours	*T* Hours	*F* Hours	*Total* Hours
5.3.X3						
before lunch	4.0	4.0	5.0	4.0	4.5	
after lunch	3.5	3.5	5.0	3.5	3.0	
12.3.X3						
before lunch	5.0	5.0	5.0	4.5	4.0	
after lunch	3.0	3.0	3.0	4.5	3.0	
19.3.X3						
before lunch	4.0	6.5	5.5	5.0	4.0	
after lunch	3.5	4.0	4.0	4.0	3.5	
26.3.X3						
before lunch	5.0	5.0	4.0	6.0	6.0	
after lunch	4.5	4.0	4.0	4.0	4.0	
	32.5	35.0	35.5	35.5	32.0	170.5

(f)

STORES RECORD CARD

Material: Lentils, 100 kg sack Maximum Quantity:

Code: Minimum Quantity:

Date	Receipts				Issues				Stock		
	G.R.N. No.	Quantity	Unit Price £	Amount £	Material Req. No.	Quantity	Unit Price £	Amount £	Quantity	Unit Price £	Amount £
1/3		4	84.00	336.00					4	84.00	336.00
1/3						1	84.00	84.00	3	84.00	252.00
8/3						1	84.00	84.00	2	84.00	168.00
15/3						1	84.00	84.00	1	84.00	84.00
22/3						1	84.00	84.00	-		

STORES RECORD CARD

Material: Vegetables, 50 kg drum Maximum Quantity: ....

Code: .... Minimum Quantity: ....

Date	Receipts				Issues				Stock		
	G.R.N. No.	Quantity	Unit Price £	Amount £	Material Req. No.	Quantity	Unit Price £	Amount £	Quantity	Unit Price £	Amount £
1/3		10	53.50	535.00					10	53.50	535.00
1/3						1	53.50	53.50	9	53.50	481.50
3/3						3	53.50	160.50	6	53.50	321.00
8/3						5	53.50	267.50	1	53.50	53.50
12/3		11	53.75	591.25					12	53.73	644.75
15/3						4	53.73	214.92	8	53.73	429.83
22/3						5	53.73	268.65	3	53.73	161.18

(g) Vegetables

These are used in the curry, of which 5,000 portions were made.

5,000 portions should have used (× 0.167 kg)	835 kgs
but did use (18 drums from stores ledger account × 50 kgs)	900 kgs
Usage variance (in kgs)	65 kgs (A)
× standard price per kg (from standard cost card)	× £1.12
Usage variance (in £)	£72.80 (A)

(h) During the four-week period the following overheads were absorbed (production volume × OAR per hour × time to produce one portion).

		£
Chilli department:	$5,300 \times £10.11 \times {}^{1.5}/_{60}$ =	1,339.58
Curry department:	$5,000 \times £8.45 \times {}^{2}/_{60}$ =	1,408.33
		2,747.91

Overheads incurred are as follows.

		£
Supervisor:	$£16,000 \times {}^{1}/_{13}$	1,230.77
Storekeeper:	$£12,000 \times {}^{1}/_{13}$	923.08
Cleaners:	$2 \times £10 \times 5$ days $\times$ 4 weeks	400.00
Heat and light:	per invoice	629.62
Overtime premium:	see workings	43.50
		3,226.97

Overheads have been under absorbed by £(3,226.97 – 2,747.91) = £479.06

Workings

1 Calculation of overtime hours worked by Fred Jarvis (using working from (e))

Week ending	*M* Hours	*T* Hours	*W* Hours	*T* Hours	*F* Hours	*Total* Hours
5.3.X3	–	–	2.0	–	–	
12.3.X3	–	–	–	1.0	–	
19.3.X3	–	2.5	1.5	1.0	–	
26.3.X3	1.5	1.0	–	2.0	2.0	
	1.5	3.5	3.5	4.0	2.0	14.5

2 Total overtime worked:

Fred Jarvix (from working 1)	14.50	hrs
Ali Khan (as given)	7.25	hrs
	21.75	hrs
× overtime premium per hour	× £2	
Overtime premium payable	£43.50	

Schedule of queries

	Query	*Action*
(a)	How do I allocate the cost of the factory supervisor?	Speak to supervisor
(b)	Labour hours are highly erratic. How does this tie in with stores and supervisor?	Speak to managing director
(c)	Why does invoice no. 7321 from Exotic Foods not agree with what was delivered?	Telephone supplier
(d)	Why was the heat and light invoice much greater than anticipated? The estimate in the business plan was for £5,000 per annum, ie £385 approximately for each of the 13 four-week periods. The actual invoiced cost for the period was £629.62.	Speak to supervisor
(e)	Why did Ali take so much longer than expected to produce the 5,300 portions of chilli?	Speak to supervisor
(f)	Some stocks need reordering	Check that they have been reordered

ANSWERS TO AAT SAMPLE SIMULATION

DO NOT TURN THIS PAGE UNTIL YOU HAVE COMPLETED THE SAMPLE SIMULATION

ANSWERS TO AAT SAMPLE SIMULATION: POLYCOT LTD

Task 1

STORES LEDGER ACCOUNT

Material description: *Plastic poppers, boxes of 100*

Code no: *PP29*

Maximum quantity: *180*
Minimum quantity: *62*
Reorder level: *95*
Reorder quantity: *100*

Date	Receipts			Issues			Stock balance		
	Quantity	Price per box £	Total £	Quantity	Price per box £	Total £	Quantity	Price per box £	Total £
1 March							75	62.50	4,687.50
2 March	100	63.70	6,370.00				75	62.50	4,687.50
							100	63.70	6,370.00
							175		11,057.50
6 March				75	62.50	4,687.50			
				15	63.70	955.50			
				90		5,643.00	85	63.70	5,414.50
9 March	100	64.40	6,440.00				85	63.70	5,414.50
							100	64.40	6,440.00
							185		11,854.50
12 March	100	66.50	6,650.00				85	63.70	5,414.50
							100	64.40	6,440.00
							100	66.50	6,650.00
							285		18,504.50
20 March				85	63.70	5,414.50	75	64.40	4,830.00
				25	64.40	1,610.00	100	66.50	6,650.00
				110		7,024.50	175		11,480.00

STORES LEDGER ACCOUNT

Material description: *Cotton, 50m rolls*

Code no: *C733*

Maximum quantity: 175
Minimum quantity: 55
Reorder level: 75
Reorder quantity: 90

Date	Receipts			Issues			Stock balance		
	Quantity	Price per roll £	Total £	Quantity	Price per roll £	Total £	Quantity	Price per roll £	Total £
1 March							65	85.50	5,557.50
6 March	90	86.80	7,812.00				65	85.50	5,557.50
							90	86.80	7,812.00
							155		13,369.50
10 March				50	85.50	4,275.00	15	85.50	1,282.50
							90	86.80	7,812.00
							105		9,094.50
12 March	90	88.20	7,938.00				15	85.50	1,282.50
							90	86.80	7,812.00
							90	88.20	7,938.00
							195		17,032.50
18 March				15	85.50	1,282.50	65	86.80	5,642.00
				25	86.80	2,170.00	90	88.20	7,938.00
				40		3,452.50	155		13,580.00
30 March				30	86.80	2,604.00	35	86.80	3,038.00
							90	88.20	7,938.00
							125		10,976.00

Task 2

MEMO

To: Patrick McGrath
From: Lesley Hunt
Date: 3 April 1998
Subject: Stock levels during March

During March the stock levels of both plastic poppers (PP29) and 50 metre cotton rolls (C733) exceeded their maximum levels.

In the case of the cotton, stock of 195 rolls was held between 12 March and 18 March (maximum level: 175 rolls).

In the case of the plastic poppers, the maximum level is 180 boxes but this was exceeded on 9 March when a new delivery brought stocks up to 185. The situation became worse on 12 March when a delivery of a further 100 boxes was received. Clearly we should never have placed this additional order: the usual reorder level is 95 boxes.

I recommend that in future we should institute more thorough checks before orders are placed with suppliers and in particular a check to ensure that the reorder level has been reached.

Task 3

TIMESHEET

Week ending 6 March 1998

Employee name Amy Harding **Employee number** 2173

Department Finishing **Employee grade** 2

Activity	Monday Hours	Tuesday Hours	Wednes-day Hours	Thursday Hours	Friday Hours	Total Hours
Machining	7	10	4		4	25
Holiday			4	8		12
Waiting for work	1					1
Training					4	4
Total hours payable for day	8	10	8	8	8	42
Number of covers produced	65	72	30	0	32	
Bonus payable @ £0.15 per cover above 60 per day	£0.75	£1.80	-	-	-	£2.55

Signed Amy Harding Manager Jim Stubbs

Analysis for week	Hours	Rate per hour £	Wages cost £
Direct wages	25	3.00	75.00
Indirect wages			
Basic hours	17	3.00	51.00
Overtime premium	1	3.00	3.00
Bonus	-	-	2.55
	43		131.55

TIMESHEET

Week ending *6 March 1998*

Employee name *Jane Amber* **Employee number** *2487*

Department *Cutting* **Employee grade** *1*

Activity	**Monday Hours**	**Tuesday Hours**	**Wednes -day Hours**	**Thursday Hours**	**Friday Hours**	**Total Hours**
Cutting	*10*	*6*	*6*		*8*	*30*
Waiting for work		*3*	*2*			*5*
Sick				*8*		*8*
Training					*2*	*2*
Discrepancy		*(1)*				*(1)*
Total hours payable for day	*10*	*8*	*8*	*8*	*10*	*44*
Number of covers produced	*70*	*51*	*62*	*0*	*62*	
Bonus payable @ £0.15 per cover above 60 per day	*£1.50*	-	*£0.30*	-	*£0.30*	*£2.10*

Signed *Jane Amber* Manager *Jim Stubbs*

Analysis for week	**Hours**	**Rate per hour**	**Wages cost**
		£	£
Direct wages	*29*	*4.00*	*116.00*
Indirect wages			
Basic hours	*15*	*4.00*	*60.00*
Overtime premium	*2*	*4.00*	*8.00*
Bonus	-	-	*2.10*
	46		*186.10*

COST LEDGER DATA ENTRY SHEET

Week ending *6 March 1998*

Debit accounts

Cost centre code	Expenditure code	Amount to be debited £
C100	E300	116.00
C200	E300	75.00
C300	E300	-
C400	E300	-
C100	E310	70.10
C200	E310	56.55
C300	E310	-
C400	E310	-

Check total: total wages for the two employees 317.65

Task 4

MEMO

To: Jim Stubbs
From: Lesley Hunt
Date: 10 March 1998
Subject: Discrepancy on timesheet

I have a query on an employee's timesheet for the week ending 6 March 1998. The employee in question is Jane Amber, in the cutting department. A copy of the timesheet is enclosed.

You will see that I have had to adjust for a discrepancy of one hour. The total number of hours shown for Tuesday is eight, but the analysis totals to nine hours.

Could you please look into this for me? I have made the usual adjustments, pending the outcome of your enquiries. Thanks for your help.

Task 5

MEMO

To: Jim Stubbs, production manager
From: Lesley Hunt, accounts assistant
Date: 10 March 1998
Subject: Standard rates for overhead absorption, 1998/99

Why the present absorption rate might not be the most appropriate for the company

The present system of absorbing production overheads using a percentage of direct labour cost may distort the overhead costs absorbed by individual products because of differential wage rates.

Our employees are paid different hourly rates. If a cost unit happens to be worked on by a highly paid employee its labour cost would be higher and the overhead absorbed would therefore also be higher. However the overhead actually incurred by this product would not necessarily be high, particularly if the higher paid employees work more quickly.

Many overhead costs tend to increase with time, for example rent, rates, salaries and so on. Therefore it makes sense to absorb overheads according to the time taken on a cost unit. Although a labour cost percentage is to an extent time based, it can lead to distortions when there are differential wage rates.

The hourly rates suggested would be preferable because the overhead absorbed would be directly related to the time taken to produce the cost unit.

Why separate hourly rates would be more suitable

The activity in the finishing and packing departments is labour intensive. Therefore a direct labour hour rate is most appropriate in these two departments. Using a separate rate for each department would more accurately reflect the load placed by a cost unit on the facilities of each department.

The cutting department is machine intensive. Therefore many of the overhead costs are likely to be machine related (for example depreciation and maintenance) and would be linked to the amount of time spent by a cost unit on the machines. Therefore a machine hour rate is more suitable in this department.

Task 6

OVERHEAD ANALYSIS SHEET: 1998/99						
Overhead expense: primary apportionments and allocations	**Basis of allocation/ apportionment**	**Total** £	**Cutting dept** £	**Finishing dept** £	**Packing dept** £	**Stores** £
Rent and rates	Floor area	79,500	19,941	27,812	19,941	11,806
Catering	Number of employees	1,200	183	623	366	28
Machine maintenance	Quotation	45,850	25,250	5,600	11,000	4,000
Depreciation on machines	Cost of machines	13,490	7,412	1,663	3,230	1,185
Production manager's salary	Time spent	21,000	7,000	7,000	7,000	
Storekeeper's salary	Allocation	14,000				14,000
Other overheads	Even apportionment	40,000	10,000	10,000	10,000	10,000
Total of primary allocations		215,040	69,786	52,698	51,537	41,019
Re-apportion stores	No. of reqns.	———	16,404	13,692	10,923	(41,019)
Total production cost centre overhead		215,040	86,190	66,390	62,460	
Machine hours			30,750			
Direct labour hours				129,750	67,500	
Overhead absorption rate for 1998/99			£2.80	£0.51	£0.93	

Task 7a

MEMO

To: Jim Stubbs
From: Lesley Hunt
Date: 6 July 1998
Subject: Wages paid to temporary employee during the quarter ending 30 June 1998

I have been informed that £1,920 was paid to a temporary employee for 320 hours worked during the quarter ending 30 June 1998. To enable me to analyse and classify the hours worked by the employee and the wages paid, could you please provide me with the following information.

- How many of the 320 hours were worked on direct tasks, and how many were worked on indirect tasks? This will help me to determine the correct expenditure code for the wages payment.

- How many hours were worked in each of the three departments? This will help me to determine the correct cost centre code, and to complete the analysis of labour hours for the period.

Thank you for your help.

Working sheet for calculation of overhead under/over absorbed

Packing department, quarter ending 30 June 1998

7(b) Production overhead absorbed (using direct labour hour rate)	18,300 × £0.93	£17,019
7(c) Actual production overhead incurred	£855 + £4,045 + £10,800 + £800	£16,500
7(d) Production overhead under or over absorbed, to be transferred to profit and loss account		£519 over absorbed

Task 8

STANDARD COST CARD 1998/99

Product: Box of 6 double duvet covers
Product code no: 00214

Description	**Material code no/direct labour grade**	**Quantity**	**Std price** £ per metre/ hour etc		**Total** £
Direct materials					
Cotton fabric	CT33	38.2 metres	1.85		70.67
Plastic poppers	PP29	60	0.67		40.20
Polyester thread	TP72	22 metres	0.00142		0.03
Packing - cardboard box	PB03	1 box	0.25		0.25
Other materials	Various	-	-		0.81
Subtotal, direct materials				(A)	111.96
Direct labour					
Cutting	Grade 1	0.35 hours	4.20		1.47
Finishing	Grade 1	4.10 hours	4.20		17.22
Packing	Grade 3	0.50 hours	2.63		1.31
Subtotal, direct labour				(B)	20.00
Production overhead					
Cutting department		1.80 machine hours	2.80		5.04
Finishing department		4.10 labour hours	0.51		2.09
Packing department		0.50 labour hours	0.93		0.46
Subtotal, production overhead				(C)	7.59
Total standard production cost				(A + B + C)	139.55

Task 9

MEMO

To: Patrick McGrath
From: Lesley Hunt
Date: 13 July 1998
Subject: Standard cost report - double duvet covers in Cutting department

As you requested, here is my interim report on the cost variances for week ended 8 July 1998.

	Favourable	*Adverse*
	£	£
Cotton price variance		568
Cotton usage variance		268
Direct labour rate variance		24
Direct labour efficiency variance	55	
Fixed overhead expenditure variance		54
Fixed overhead capacity variance		28
Fixed overhead efficiency variance		90
	£55	£1,032

Clearly the two variances that require investigation are those for usage and price of cotton. I will look into these as soon as possible, but likely explanations are as follows:

- We may have been unrealistic in setting our standards for price and usage.
- There may have been a recent price increase.
- We may have switched to a higher grade of cotton.
- Wastage levels may have increased.

Workings - variances for week ended 8/7/98 (cutting department)

Cotton price variance	£	
11,350 metres should cost (@ £1.85)	20,997	
did cost	21,565	
Variance	568	(A)
Cotton usage variance	*Metres*	
1,760 covers should require (@ 38.2/6)	11,205	
did require	11,350	
Difference	145	
@ standard price (£1.85)	£268	(A)
Direct labour rate variance	£	
90 hours should cost (@ £4.20)	378	
did cost	402	
Variance	24	(A)
Direct labour efficiency variance	Hours	
1,760 covers should require (@ 0.35/6)	103	
did require	90	
Difference	13	
@ standard rate (£4.20)	£55	(F)
Fixed overhead expenditure variance	£	
Budgeted overheads (1,900 × (1.8/6) × £2.80)	1,596	
Actual overheads	1,650	
Variance	54	(A)
Fixed overhead capacity variance	Hours	
Budgeted hours worked (1,900 × 1.8/6)	570	
Actual hours worked	560	
Difference	10	
@ standard rate (£2.80)	£28	(A)
Fixed overhead efficiency variance	Hours	
Standard hours (1,760 × 1.8/6)	528	
Actual hours	560	
Difference	32	
@ standard rate (£2.80)	£90	(A)

Answers to trial run central assessments

ANSWERS TO TRIAL RUN CENTRAL ASSESSMENT 1

DO NOT TURN THIS PAGE UNTIL YOU HAVE COMPLETED TRIAL RUN CENTRAL ASSESSMENT 1

RECORDING COST INFORMATION (RCI)

ANSWERS

SECTION 1

Task 1.1

STOCK CARD Product: New World Red								
	Receipts					Issues	Balance	
Date	Quantity	Actual Cost (per bottle) £	Total Actual Cost £	Total Standard Cost £	Price Variance* £	Quantity	Quantity	Total Standard Cost £
B/f at 1 May	100			500.00			100	500.00
2 May	240	5.20	1,248.00	1,200.00	48.00 (A)		340	1,700.00
7 May						300	40	200.00
9 May	180	5.30	954.00	900.00	54.00 (A)		220	1,100.00
14 May						200	20	100.00
16 May	360	5.00	1,800.00	1,800.00	-		380	1,900.00
21 May						230	150	750.00
23 May	480	4.95	2,376.00	2,400.00	24.00 (F)		630	3,150.00
28 May						120	510	2,550.00

* Price variance = total actual cost – total standard cost

Task 1.2

The total price variance is the sum of the individual price variances.

Total price variance = £48 (A) + £54 (A) – £24 (F)

= £78 (A)

Task 1.3

On 28 May there are 510 bottles of 'New World Red' in stock

	£
480 bottles @ £4.95	2,376
30 bottles @ £5.00	150
	2,526

Task 1.4

Material usage variance – 'New World Red'

1,500 evening meals should use (÷ 10)	150 bottles
but did use	100 bottles
Usage variance (in bottles)	50 (F) bottles
× standard price per bottle	£5
Usage variance (in £)	£250 (F)

Task 1.5

(a) Standard labour time for 1,500 evening meals $= 1{,}500 \times \frac{20}{60}$ hours

$= 500$ hours

Standard labour time for 1,380 breakfast meals $= 1{,}380 \times \frac{10}{60}$ hours

$= 230$ hours

Therefore, total standard labour hours for 1,380 breakfasts and 1,500 evening meals is 500 + 230 = 730 hours.

(b) Total standard labour cost for 1,380 breakfasts and 1,500 evening meals

= 730 hours × £6 per hour

= £4,380

(c)

	£
Labour costs were	5,000
but should have been	4,380
	620 (A)

(d) **Labour efficiency variance**

Evening meals and breakfasts should have taken	730 hours
but did take	800 hours
Efficiency variance in hours	70 (A) hours
× standard rate per hour	£6
Efficiency variance in £	£420 (A)

(e) **Labour wage rate variance**

	£
800 hours should have cost (× £6)	4,800
but did cost	5,000
Labour wage rate variance	200 (A)

Task 1.6

STANDARD DIRECT COST REPORT (EXTRACT) Period: Four weeks ended 28 May 2000		
Description	**Favourable Variance** £	**Adverse Variance** £
BAR		
'New World Red' price variance		78.00
KITCHEN		
'New World Red' usage variance	250.00	
Labour efficiency variance		420.00
Labour wage rate variance		200.00

COMMENTS

Adverse price variance

From the stock card, it seems that the cost per bottle varies with the number of bottles purchased. When 360 bottles are purchased, the actual cost per bottle is the same as the standard cost, £5. When 480 bottles are purchased, the cost per bottle falls to £4.95 per bottle. It therefore appears that quantity discounts are available when orders are of a certain size.

It may not always be possible to purchase large quantities of wine, and this is when adverse price variances will arise ie, if cash flow restrictions are in force, or if there are problems with regular suppliers.

Favourable usage variance

This variance may have arisen if the bar did not supply the required quantities of wine to the kitchen.

It is also possible that the kitchen meals prepared required less than the amount of wine allowed for in the standard.

Adverse labour efficiency variance

This variance may be due to inefficient workings in the kitchen. It is also possible that the demand for meals was lower than expected – if labour costs are fixed, kitchen staff will be paid whether they are preparing meals or not.

Adverse labour wage rate variance

The actual labour wage rate was £0.25 more per hour than the standard labour wage rate. The most likely reason for this wage rate variance is because kitchen staff were required to work overtime. Alternatively, staff being paid more than £6 per hour might have been required to help out in the kitchen. It is also possible that wage rises occurred which were not anticipated when the standards were prepared.

SECTION 2

Task 2.1

Overhead	Basis	Total £	Accommodation £	Restaurant £	Bar £	Kitchen £	Administration £
Bedroom repairs	Allocated	2,400.00	2,400.00				
Electricity	Metered	1,350.00	450.00	200.00	50.00	600.00	50.00
Rent	Floor space	12,000.00	7,200.00	2,400.00	1,200.00	600.00	600.00
Kitchen repairs	Allocated	580.00				580.00	
Staff costs	Allocated	13,110.00	2,200.00	4,200.00	1,500.00		5,210.00
Other property overheads	Floor space	2,800.00	1,680.00	560.00	280.00	140.00	140.00
		32,240.00	13,930.00	7,360.00	3,030.00	1,920.00	6,000.00
Administration			4,200.00	600.00	600.00	600.00	(6,000.00)
		32,240.00	18,130.00	7,960.00	3,630.00	2,520.00	–

Task 2.2

Breakfast

Budgeted direct labour hours $= 5 \text{ staff} \times 2 \text{ hours} \times 7 \text{ days} \times 4 \text{ weeks}$

$= 280$ hours

Evening meals

Budgeted direct labour hours $= 5 \text{ staff} \times 4 \text{ hours} \times 7 \text{ days} \times 4 \text{ weeks}$

$= 560$ hours

$\therefore$ Total budgeted direct labour hours $= 280 + 560$

$= 840$ hours

Task 2.3

$$\text{Budgeted labour hour overhead absorption rate} = \frac{\text{Budgeted Kitchen Overheads}}{\text{Budgeted labour hours in the kitchen}}$$

$$= \frac{£2{,}520}{840}$$

$= £3$ per labour hour

Task 2.4

Breakfast

If it takes 10 minutes to prepare each breakfast, then 6 breakfasts can be prepared in one hour. (60 minutes ÷ 10 minutes = 6).

Therefore, overhead absorption cost per breakfast $= \frac{£3}{6} = £0.50$.

Evening meal

If it takes 20 minutes to prepare each evening meal, then 3 evening meals can be prepared in one hour. (60 minutes ÷ 20 minutes = 3).

Therefore, overhead absorption cost per evening meal $= \frac{£3}{3} = £1.00$.

Task 2.5

STANDARD INDIRECT COST REPORT

Cost centre: Kitchen

Period: Four weeks ended 28 May 2000

Description	**Favourable Variance** **£**	**Adverse Variance** **£**
Fixed overhead expenditure variance	420.00	
Fixed overhead volume variance		330.00
Fixed overhead capacity variance		120.00
Fixed overhead efficiency variance		210.00

COMMENTS

Favourable fixed overhead expenditure variance

This variance may have arisen because some overheads may not be totally fixed, for example, electricity costs. Consequently, if levels of activity are lower than budgeted, then overhead expenditure will also be lower.

Adverse fixed overhead volume variance

This variance may have arisen because the demand for meals was less than expected. It is important to establish the reason for this – and management should be assured that it is not as a result of poor quality meals being served.

Adverse fixed overhead capacity and efficiency variances

These variances indicate that the kitchen is not being run very efficiently compared with standard and also that the hours worked in the kitchen in this period were below full capacity.

These variances are sub-variances of the fixed overhead volume variance.

Workings

Fixed overhead expenditure variance

	£
Budgeted fixed overhead expenditure	2,520
Actual fixed overhead expenditure	2,100
	420 (F)

Fixed overhead volume variance

	£
Actual production at standard rate*	2,190
Budgeted production at standard rate	2,520
Fixed overhead volume variance	330 (A)

		£
* 1,500 evening meals at £1 each	=	1,500
1,380 breakfasts at £0.50 each	=	690
		2,190

Fixed overhead capacity variance

Budgeted hours of work	840 hours
Actual hours of work	800 hours
Fixed overhead capacity variance in hours	40 hours (A)
× standard overhead absorption rate	£3
Fixed overhead capacity variance in £	£120 (A)

Fixed overhead efficiency variance

Efficiency variance (in hours) as per task 1.5	70 hours (A)
× standard overhead absorption rate per hour	£3
	£210 (A)

ANSWERS TO TRIAL RUN CENTRAL ASSESSMENT 2

DO NOT TURN THIS PAGE UNTIL YOU HAVE COMPLETED TRIAL RUN CENTRAL ASSESSMENT 2

SECTION 1

Task 1.1

Total quantity of PCBs purchased = 71,500 units
Total price paid for all purchases = £361,000

	£	
71,500 units should have cost (× £4.50)	321,750	
but did cost	361,000	
Total price variance	39,250	(A)

Task 1.2

Standard usage = 35,000 units produced × 2 PCBs per unit = 70,000 PCBs

Task 1.3

	PCBs Units
Opening stocks	35,000
Purchases	71,500
Closing stocks	(32,000)
PCBs used	74,500

Usage variance

35,000 units produced should have used (× 2)	70,000	Units
but did use	74,500	Units
Usage variance in units	4,500	Units (A)
× standard price per unit of PCB	× £4.50	
Usage variance in £	£20,250	(A)

Task 1.4

Buffer stock = 8,000 units × 2 PCBs = 16,000 units of PCB

Reorder level = Buffer stock + (budgeted (maximum) usage × maximum lead time)

= 16,000 +(16,000 × 2) = 48,000 units of PCB

Task 1.5

(a) Standard labour time to assemble total production = 35,000 units × 0.25 hrs
= 8,750 hours

(b) Standard labour cost for total production = 35,000 units × £1
= £35,000

(c)

	£	
35,000 units produced should cost (× £1)	35,000	
but did cost	38,775	
Total labour cost variance	3,775	(A)

(d)

35,000 units produced should have taken (× 0.25 hr)	8,750	Hrs
but did take	8,250	Hrs
Efficiency variance in hours	500	Hrs (F)
× standard rate per hour	× £4	
Labour efficiency variance in £	£2,000	(F)

(e)

	£	
8,250 hours should have cost (× £4)	33,000	
but did cost	38,775	
Labour wage rate variance	5,775	(A)

Task 1.6

STANDARD DIRECT COST REPORT (EXTRACT)

Period: November 2000

Description	Favourable Variance (£)	Adverse Variance (£)
PCB price variance		39,250
PCB usage variance		20,250
S100 labour efficiency variance	2,000	
S100 labour wage rate variance		5,775

PCB price variance

The adverse price variance indicates that the average price paid for PCBs was higher than the standard price of £4.50 per unit. If this was not due to careless purchasing then the variance may be unavoidable and consideration should be given to increasing the standard price next year.

However, the analysis of purchase invoices reveals that the standard price of £4.50 was paid, when the largest batch of 20,000 units was ordered. Mobiles Ltd seems to order a different quantity each time, and the supplier's price appears to depend on the quantity ordered.

In order to establish a realistic standard price for next year, Mobiles Ltd needs to establish the economic order quantity, taking account of the holding costs, ordering costs, and discounts available for purchasing larger quantities. Once the reorder quantity has been established, the supplier's pricing structure will help to indicate the correct standard price.

If Mobiles Ltd wishes to maintain the standard price at or close to £4.50 per unit, it may be necessary to approach other suppliers in order to introduce an element of competition into the suppliers' tendering process.

PCB usage variance

The adverse usage variance indicates that, on average, more than two PCBs are being used for each S100 produced. If investigations reveal that this was due to unavoidable wastage and rejections then consideration may be given to increasing the standard usage allowance for next year.

However, management may have deliberately set an ideal standard so that the resulting adverse variances highlight the cost of rejections. In this case the standard may not require alteration.

S100 labour efficiency variance

The favourable efficiency variance indicates that the average time taken per unit produced was less than the time allowed. If this is the result of efficiencies which can be continued, perhaps through the discovery of new working methods, then the standard time allowance should be reduced in next year's standard.

However, investigation of the variance may not reveal any efficiencies which can be repeated, in which case the standard time allowance would not be altered. Perhaps more highly skilled employees were used (hence the adverse wage rate variance) but this practice might not be continued in future.

S100 wage rate variance

The adverse variance indicates that the average hourly rate paid was higher than standard. This may be because more highly skilled employees were used (see above). If this practice is to be continued then the standard hourly rate should be increased for next year.

Alternatively, the adverse variance may indicate that inflationary increases in wage rates need to be reflected in an updated standard hourly rate for labour.

Performance standards

In determining the material and labour cost standards, an agreed performance level would have been used. Three types of **performance standard** are ideal, attainable and basic standards.

Ideal standards are based on the most favourable operating conditions, with no allowance for wastage and other inefficiencies. It is probable that the standard usage of PCBs was set on this basis, but such standards can have an unfavourable motivational impact.

Attainable standards are based on efficient operating conditions. Some allowance is made for wastage and other inefficiencies. If well-set these standards provide a useful psychological incentive, and for this reason they should be used whenever possible.

Basic standards are kept unaltered over a long period of time. They are used to show changes in efficiency or performance over an extended time period. However, basic cost standards are likely to be out of date and are therefore seldom used.

Task 2.1

	Actual	*Budget*	*Variance*
	£	£	£
Supervisors' wages	5,600	5,200	400 (A)
Rent and rates	24,400	24,000	400 (A)
Buildings insurance	2,850	3,000	150 (F)
Power	7,240	6,800	440 (A)
Heat and light	6,250	6,000	250 (A)
Consumable materials	22,160	18,750	3,410 (A)
Depreciation of machinery	30,000	30,000	-
Total	98,500	93,750	4,750 (A)

Task 2.2

(a) Budgeted direct labour hour overhead absorption rate =

$$\frac{£93{,}750}{12{,}500} = £7.50 \text{ per direct labour hour}$$

(b)

	£	
Actual production at standard rate (12,200 × £7.50)	91,500	
Budgeted production at standard rate (12,500 × £7.50)	93,750	
Overhead volume variance	2,250	(A)

(c)

Actual production achieved should take	12,200	Hrs
But did take	13,850	Hrs
Overhead efficiency variance in hours	1,650	Hrs (A)
× standard overhead absorption rate per hour	× £7.50	
Overhead efficiency variance in £	£12,375	(A)

(d)

Budgeted hours of work	12,500	Hrs
Actual hours of work	13,850	Hrs
Overhead capacity variance in hours	1,350	Hrs (F)
× standard overhead absorption rate per hour	× £7.50	
Overhead capacity variance in £	£10,125	(F)

Task 2.3

(a)

	Dr £	Cr £
Finished goods stocks (12,200 std hrs × £7.50)	91,500	
Fixed overhead expenditure variance	4,750	
Fixed overhead volume variance	2,250	
Fixed overhead control - assembly		98,500

(b) The **adverse fixed overhead expenditure** variance represents the overhead under-absorbed as a result of the actual expenditure being higher than the budgeted expenditure.

The **adverse fixed overhead volume variance** represents the overhead under-absorbed as a result of the actual output volume being lower than the budgeted volume.

At the end of the month both adverse variances will be debited in the profit and loss account. They will be added to the standard cost of sales for the month.

If the variances are significant it may be necessary to apportion part of them to the value of stock at the end of the month. This is because the stock would be under-valued if it was priced at standard cost, when significant variances exist.

Task 2.4

	NOVEMBER RESULTS	BUDGETED ACTIVITY (Direct labour hours)	
Direct labour hours	13,850	14,000	15,000
	Base Cost	**Budgeted Cost**	**Budgeted Cost**
	£	**£**	**£**
Supervisors' wages	5,600	5,600	5,600
Rent and rates	24,400	24,400	24,400
Buildings insurance	2,850	2,850	2,850
Power	7,240	7,240	7,240
Heat and light	6,250	6,250	6,250
Consumable materials	22,160	22,400*	24,000*
Depreciation of machinery	30,000	30,000	30,000
Total	**98,500**	98,740	100,340

* $\frac{£22{,}160}{13{,}850} = £1.60$ per direct labour hour

14,000 direct labour hours × £1.60 = £22,400

15,000 direct labour hours × £1.60 = £24,000

Task 2.5

An increase in activity will reduce the **fixed** overhead absorption rate per direct labour hour. This is because the same total fixed overhead will be divided by a higher number of labour hours. This will consequently **reduce the fixed overhead cost** to be charged to an individual product.

An increase in activity will not affect the amount of **variable overhead cost** charged to an individual product. This is because the amount of variable overhead cost will increase in line with the increase in activity.

Task 2.6

REPORT

To: Managing director, Mobiles Ltd

From: Accounting technician

Subject: Standard fixed overhead absorption rates

Date: XX.XX.XX

In order to establish a standard fixed overhead absorption rate for the forthcoming year, it will be necessary to determine two items: the **budgeted fixed overhead expenditure** and the **budgeted activity level**, in terms of direct labour hours. The standard fixed overhead absorption rate will be calculated as:

$$\text{Fixed overhead absorption rate} = \frac{\text{budgeted fixed overhead expenditure}}{\text{budgeted activity level}}$$

Budgeted fixed overhead expenditure

The information in task 2.1 indicates that expenditure was higher than budget for all fixed overhead cost items, apart from buildings insurance and depreciation. Each item will need to be reviewed separately, but the adverse variances may indicate the necessity to increase the budgeted expenditure to allow for inflation.

Budgeted activity level

The information in task 2.2 indicates that the volume variance was adverse. This suggests that Mobile Ltd may need to revise their budgeted activity level downwards.

The adverse volume variance was caused by adverse efficiency, resulting in a **potential shortfall in output**. Since the labour efficiency variance on the S100 was favourable, this points to significant adverse efficiency on other products, outweighing this favourable effect. The standard time allowances need to be reviewed to see if they are still realistic targets for the forthcoming year in the light of current working practices.

The capacity variance was favourable, indicating that it is **possible to operate at a higher level of activity**, in terms of labour hours, than was included in the original budget. This can be taken into account when projecting the activity level for next year, but of course the budgeted output (activity) will depend on Mobile Ltd's forecast sales level.

ANSWERS TO TRIAL RUN CENTRAL ASSESSMENT 3

DO NOT TURN THIS PAGE UNTIL YOU HAVE COMPLETED TRIAL RUN CENTRAL ASSESSMENT 3

SECTION 1

Task 1.1

STOCK CARD

Product: **Motor oil**

Standard price: **£1 per litre**

Centre: **Servicing**

	Receipts					**Issues**	**Balance**	
Date	**Quantity** litres	**Actual cost per litre** £	**Total actual cost** £	**Total standard cost** £	**Price variance** £	**Quantity** litres	**Quantity** litres	**Total standard cost** £
B/f 1 May							2,100	2,100
4 May	2,400	1.20	2,880	2,400	480 (A)		4,500	4,500
8 May						3,300	1,200	1,200
10 May	3,000	1.10	3,300	3,000	300 (A)		4,200	4,200
11 May						3,200	1,000	1,000
17 May	5,000	1.00	5,000	5,000	–		6,000	6,000
18 May						5,400	600	600
23 May	6,400	0.95	6,080	6,400	320 (F)		7,000	7,000
24 May						4,420	2,580	2,580

Task 1.2

Total material price variance = £480 (A) + £300 (A) – £320 (F) = £460 (A)

Task 1.3

(a)

	Dr	Cr
	£	**£**
Motor oil stocks	16,800	
Material price variance	460	
Creditors' control account		17,260

(b) The material price variance is most likely to be debited in the profit and loss account to increase the material cost of production.

Task 1.4

(a) **Standard usage of motor oil**

Each completed oil service uses 10 litres.

Therefore, standard usage for 1,420 oil services = 1,420 × 10 litres = 14,200 litres

(b) **Material usage variance**

1,420 oil services should use	14,200 litres
but did use	16,320 litres
Material usage variance (in litres)	2,120 litres (A)
× standard price per litre	× £1
Material usage variance (in £)	£2,120 (A)

(c) **Standard labour time**

Each completed oil service should take 0.75 hours. Therefore 1,420 oil services should take 1,420 × 0.75 = 1,065 hours.

(d) **Standard labour cost**

Standard labour cost = Standard labour time × standard labour rate per hour
= 1,065 hours × £10 per hour
= £10,650

(e) **Labour efficiency variance**

1,420 oil services should take (× 0.75 hours)	1,065 hours
but did take	1,250 hours
Labour efficiency variance (in hours)	185 hours (A)
× standard rate per hour	× £10
Labour efficiency variance (in £)	£1,850 (A)

(f) **Labour rate variance**

	£
1,250 hours should cost (× £10)	12,500
but did cost	10,850
Labour rate variance	1,650 (F)

Task 1.5

(a)

	Dr	Cr
	£	£
Cost of sales	10,650	
Labour efficiency variance	1,850	
Labour rate variance		1,650
Wages control account		10,850

(b) The labour efficiency variance (£1,850 (A)) will be debited to the profit and loss account and the labour rate variance (£1,650 (F)) will be credited to the profit and loss account. The net effect of recording these variances in the profit and loss account will be to increase expenditure by £200 and to reduce profits by the same amount.

Task 1.6

REPORT

To:	**Finance Director**	**From:**	A Technician
Subject:	Variance analysis	**Date:**	June 2001

Material price variance - £460 (A)

The standard price of motor oil is £1 per litre. The actual price per litre when 5,000 litres are purchased is also £1 per litre. However when smaller quantities (ie less than 5,000 litres) are purchased, the price per litre increases.

Similarly, when quantities greater than 5,000 litres are purchased, the actual price per litre is less than £1. Such variations from the standard price of £1 per litre lead to both adverse and favourable material price variances.

Material usage variance - £2,120 (A)

The standard usage of 10 litres of motor oil per oil service applies to all engine sizes. Smaller engines are likely to give rise to an oil requirement of less than 10 litres (and hence a favourable usage variance).

Similarly, larger engines are likely to give rise to an oil requirement of more than 10 litres (and hence an adverse usage variance). An overall adverse usage variance suggests that more services (than expected) were carried out on larger engines.

Labour rate variance - £1,650 (F)

A favourable labour rate variance suggests that the actual hourly rate was less than the standard rate. This may be because a less skilled labour force was employed at a lower hourly rate.

Labour efficiency variance - £1,850 (A)

If the workforce employed were less skilled than expected (as suggested above) this could lead to an adverse labour efficiency variance (since the workforce would be less efficient than expected).

SECTION 2

Task 2.1

Fixed overhead	Basis	Total	New car sales	Used car sales	Servicing	Admin.
		£	£	£	£	£
Depreciation	Net book value	7,200	1,200	1,200	4,000	800
Rent	Floor space	20,000	8,000	6,000	4,000	2,000
Other property overheads	Floor space	11,500	4,600	3,450	2,300	1,150
Fixed staff costs	Allocated	169,710	62,100	54,200	28,200	25,210
Administration overheads	Allocated	25,840				25,840
		234,250	75,900	64,850	38,500	55,000
Administration	Apportioned		11,000	16,500	27,500	(55,000)
		234,250	86,900	81,350	66,000	–

Task 2.2

(a) **Standard fixed overhead absorption rate per direct labour hour**

$$= \frac{\text{Servicing department overheads}}{\text{Budgeted direct labour hours}}$$

$$= \frac{\text{£66,000}}{\text{8,250 direct labour hours}}$$

= £8 per direct labour hour

(b) **Fixed overhead expenditure variance**

	£	
Budgeted fixed overhead expenditure	66,000	
Actual fixed overhead expenditure	72,540	
Fixed overhead expenditure variance	6,540	(A)

(c) **Fixed overhead volume variance**

Actual production volume achieved	8,100	hours
Budgeted production volume	8,250	hours
Volume variance (in hours)	150	(A) hours
× standard absorption rate per hour	× £8	
Fixed overhead volume variance	1,200	(A)

(d) **Fixed overhead efficiency variance**

Standard hours produced	8,100	hours
Direct labour hours worked	8,500	hours
	400	(A) hours
× standard absorption rate per hour	× £8	
Fixed overhead efficiency variance	£3,200	(A)

(e) **Fixed overhead capacity variance**

Budgeted direct labour hours	8,250	hours
Actual direct labour hours	8,500	hours
Fixed overhead capacity variance (in hours)	250	(F) hours
× standard absorption rate per hour	× £8	
Fixed overhead capacity variance (in £)	£2,000	(F)

Task 2.3

Servicing	**Budgeted activity (labour hours)**		
	8,250	**9,075**	**9,900**
Budgeted fixed overheads	**May 2001** **£**	**£**	**£**
Depreciation	4,000	4,000	5,400
Rent	4,000	4,000	4,000
Other property overheads	2,300	6,300	6,300
Staff costs	28,200	28,200	28,200
Administration	27,500	27,500	27,500
Total	66,000	70,000	71,400
Standard overhead absorption rate (rounded to nearest penny)	£8.00	£7.71	£7.21

Task 2.4

(a)

Activity level	**£**
8,250 labour hours	0.75 hours × £8.00 = £6.00
9,075 labour hours	0.75 hours × £7.71 = £5.78
9,900 labour hours	0.75 hours × £7.21 = £5.41

(b) **Efficiency ratio** $= \dfrac{\text{expected hours to make output}}{\text{actual hours taken}} \times 100\%$

$$= \frac{8{,}100 \text{ hours}}{8{,}500 \text{ hours}} \times 100\%$$

= 95.29% (to 2 decimal places)

Capacity ratio $= \dfrac{\text{Actual hours worked}}{\text{Hours budgeted}} \times 100\%$

$$= \frac{8{,}500 \text{ hours}}{8{,}250 \text{ hours}} \times 100\%$$

= 103.03% (to 2 decimal places)

Task 2.5

REPORT

To: Finance Director **From:** Accounting Technician

Subject: Fixed overhead and capacity levels **Date:** June 2001

(a) **Fixed overhead cost of oil change**

The standard fixed overhead absorption rate per direct labour hour was calculated to be £8 (see task 2.2 (a)). The standard time to complete an oil change is 0.75 hours.

Therefore, the fixed overhead cost of an oil change = 0.75 hours × £8 = £6 per oil change.

(b) **Revision of standard fixed overhead absorption rate**

Since actual fixed overhead expenditure was £6,540 higher than budgeted (as calculated in task 2.2) this would suggest that the standard fixed overhead absorption rate should be increased to prevent under absorption of overheads.

(c) **Effect of changes in activity**

The standard fixed overhead absorption rate is calculated as:

$$\frac{\text{Servicing department overheads}}{\text{Budgeted direct labour hours}}$$

If activity levels change, so too will the standard fixed overhead absorption rate. It will increase if activity levels fall, and decrease if activity levels rise.

(d) **Capacity and efficiency variances**

A capacity ratio of 103.03% indicates that the original budgets are set below the actual capacity of the department. An efficiency ratio of 95.29% indicates that the department was operating inefficiently.

ANSWERS TO DECEMBER 2001 CENTRAL ASSESSMENT

DO NOT TURN THIS PAGE UNTIL YOU HAVE COMPLETED THE DECEMBER 2001 CENTRAL ASSESSMENT

SECTION 1

Task 1.1

STOCK CARD								
Product: White cloth								
Standard cost: £2.20 per metre								
	Receipts					**Issues**	**Balance**	
Date	**Quantity** Metres	**Actual Cost (per metre)** £	**Total Actual Cost** £	**Total Standard Cost** £	**Price Variance** £	**Quantity** Metres	**Quantity** Metres	**Total Standard Cost** £
B/f at 1 Nov							60,200	132,440
4 Nov	11,400	2.50	28,500	25,080	3,420 (A)		71,600	157,520
8 Nov						24,800	46,800	102,960
10 Nov	13,000	2.40	31,200	28,600	2,600 (A)		59,800	131,560
11 Nov						18,200	41,600	91,520
17 Nov	15,200	2.30	34,960	33,440	1,520 (A)		56,800	124,960
18 Nov						15,400	41,400	91,080
23 Nov	16,600	2.25	37,350	36,520	830 (A)		58,000	127,600
30 Nov						24,480	33,520	73,744

Task 1.2

Total price variance = £3,420 (A) + £2,600 (A) + £1,520 (A) + £830 (A) = £8,370 (A)

Task 1.3

(a) 101 metres of white cloth are required in order to produce 100 metres of *Rosy Glow* fabric.

Therefore $= \frac{101\text{m}}{100\text{m}}$ = 1.01m of white cloth are required per metre of *Rosy Glow* fabric manufactured.

Therefore, the **standard usage of white cloth** for 8,500 metres of *Rosy Glow* fabric = 8,500 metres × 1.01 = 8,585 metres of white cloth.

(b) 10 litres of red dye are required in order to produce 100 metres of *Rosy Glow* fabric. Therefore 10/100 = 0.1 litres of red dye are required in order to produce one metre of *Rosy Glow* fabric.

Therefore, the **standard usage of red dye** needed to manufacture 8,500 metres of *Rosy Glow* fabric = 8,500 × 0.1 litres = 850 litres.

(c) **White cloth – material usage variance**

8,500 metres of *Rosy Glow* should use	8,585 metres
but did use	9,000 metres
Material usage variance (in metres)	415 metres (A)
× standard price per metre	£2.20
Material usage variance (in £)	913 (A)

(d) **Red dye – material usage variance**

8,500 metres of *Rosy Glow* should use	850 litres
but did use	900 litres
Material usage variance (in litres)	50 litres (A)
× standard price per litre	£8
Material usage variance (in £)	400 (A)

(e) **Standard labour time**

5 hours of direct labour are required to manufacture 100 metres of *Rosy Glow* fabric.

Therefore, $\frac{5 \text{ hours}}{100}$ = 0.05 hours or 3 minutes are required to manufacture 1 metre of *Rosy Glow* fabric.

Therefore the **standard labour time** to manufacture 8,500 metres of *Rosy Glow* fabric = 8,500 × 0.05 hours = 425 hours.

(f) **Standard labour cost**

Standard labour cost per metre = standard labour time per metre × standard labour rate

= 0.05 hours × £6

= £0.30 per metre

Therefore the **standard labour cost** for the manufacture of 8,500 metres of *Rosy Glow* fabric = 8,500 × £0.30 = £2,550.

(g) **Labour efficiency variance**

8,500 metres of *Rosy Glow* should take (× 0.05 hours)	425 hours
but did take	550 hours
Labour efficiency variance (in hours)	125 hours (A)
× standard rate per hour	£6
Labour efficiency variance (in £)	£750 (A)

(h) **Labour rate variance**

	£
550 hours should cost (× £6)	3,300.0
but did cost (550 hours × £5.25)	2,887.5
Labour rate variance	412.5 (F)

Task 1.4

REPORT

To: Finance Director
Subject: Variance analysis

From: Accounting technician
Date: 4 December 2001

Price variance for white cloth £8,370 (A)

This adverse variance might have arisen because of unforeseen increases in the price of white cloth. (It is important to update standards regularly for this reason). It is also possible that there was a change in the material standard for this fabric that caused the standard price to be decreased (unnecessarily). Another reason for this variance occurring could be that the purchasing department were careless in purchasing this material. They may have been able to pay more competitive prices if they had shopped around. Furthermore, it is noticeable that the price per metre is lower when large quantities are purchased. Bulk purchase discounts may have been forgone by purchasing smaller quantities than standard each time.

Usage variance for white cloth £913 (A)

One possible reason for this variance is that the material used was of lower quality than standard. Other reasons include the less effective use of material and errors in allocating materials to jobs.

Usage variance for red dye £400 (A)

It is possible that the red dye required to manufacture the *Rosy Glow* fabric was not up to the required standard and therefore more dye needed to be used. Similarly, there could also have been excessive waste of this dye when manufacturing the *Rosy Glow* fabric, or some of the dye could have been stolen or spilled.

Labour rate variance £412.50 (F)

One possible reason for this variance is that apprentices or lower paid workers (than standard) were used in the manufacture of this fabric.

Labour efficiency variance £750 (A)

Possible reasons for this variance include the following.

- Lack of training in the manufacture of this fabric.
- Sub-standard red dye may have been used to manufacture the *Rosy Glow* fabric, which slowed the production process.
- There may have been errors in allocating the actual time spent on the manufacture of this fabric.

Helping hand. Sometimes our answers include more than one possible reason for the variances occurring. We have included this extra information in order to help you with your revision. Remember, however, that in an assessment you would only need to state one possible reason. Make sure you read the tasks very carefully.

Task 1.5

FIFO value of stock of white cloth at 30 November 2001

At 30 November 2001, stock white cloth was 33,520 metres.

FIFO values stock at the most recent prices.

	£
16,600 metres @ £2.25	37,350
15,200 metres @ £2.30	34,960
1,720* metres @ £2.40	4,128
	76,438

* 33,520 – 16,600 – 15,200 = 1,720

The FIFO value of stock at 30 November 2001 was therefore £76,438.

SECTION 2

Task 2.1

Actual fixed overheads for November 2001	Basis	Total £	Warehouse £	Manufacturing £	Sales £	Administration £
Depreciation	Net book value	14,600	2,920	10,220	730	730
Rent	% floor space	48,000	9,600	31,200	2,400	4,800
Other property overheads	% floor space	12,800	2,560	8,320	640	1,280
Administration overheads	allocation	28,800	–	–	–	28,800
Staff costs	allocation	39,800	4,800	14,340	12,250	8,410
		144,000	19,880	64,080	16,020	44,020

Workings

Depreciation

Warehouse = $\frac{160}{800}$ × £14,600 = £2,920

Manufacturing = $\frac{560}{800}$ × £14,600 = £10,220

Sales = $\frac{40}{800}$ × £14,600 = £730

Administration = $\frac{40}{800}$ × £14,600 = £730

Rent

Warehouse = 20% × £48,000 = £9,600

Manufacturing = 65% × £48,000 = £31,200

Sales = 5% × £48,000 = £2,400

Administration = 10% × £48,000 = £4,800

> **Helping hand**. Other property overheads will be apportioned in exactly the same way as rent.

Task 2.2

Manufacturing department for November 2001	Actual fixed overheads	Budgeted fixed overheads	Variance
	£	£	£
Depreciation	10,220	9,820	400 (A)
Rent	31,200	31,200	–
Other property overheads	8,320	3,800	4,520 (A)
Staff costs	14,340	13,305	1,035 (A)
Total	64,080	58,125	5,955 (A)

Task 2.3

(a) Budgeted fixed overhead absorption rate $= \frac{\text{Budgeted fixed overheads}}{\text{Budgeted direct labour hours}}$

$= \frac{£58,125}{4,650}$

= £12.50 per direct labour hour

(b) **Overhead volume variance**

Actual production volume achieved	4,100 std hrs
Budgeted production volume	4,650 std hrs
Volume variance in std hrs	550 std hrs (A)
× standard absorption rate per hour	× 12.50
Overhead volume variance in £	£6,875 (A)

(c) **Overhead efficiency variance**

Standard direct labour hours produced	4,100 hours
Actual direct labour hours worked	4,780 hours
Overhead efficiency variance in hours	680 hours (A)
× standard overhead absorption rate per hour	× £12.50
Overhead efficiency variance in £	£8,500 (A)

(d) **Overhead capacity variance**

Budgeted direct labour hours	4,650 hours
Actual direct labour hours worked	4,780 hours
Overhead capacity variance (in hours)	130 hours (F)
× standard overhead absorption rate per hour	× £12.50
Overhead capacity variance in £	£1,625 (F)

Task 2.4

(a)

Journal	Dr £	Cr £
Finished goods stock	51,250*	
Overhead expenditure variance	5,955	
Overhead volume variance	6,875	
Overhead control – manufacturing		64,080

* Overheads absorbed = standard hours produced × standard absorption rate per hour

= 4,100 hours × £12.50

= £51,250

(b) (i) **Fixed overhead expenditure variance**

The adverse fixed overhead expenditure variance of £5,955 will be recorded as a debit in the profit and loss account. It will be added to the standard cost of sales for the month.

(ii) **Fixed overhead volume variance**

The adverse fixed overhead volume variance of £6,875 will also be recorded as a debit in the profit and loss account, and added to the standard cost of sales for the month.

If the variances are significant it may be necessary to apportion part of them to the value of stock at the end of the month. This is because the stock would be under-valued if it was priced at standard cost, when significant variances exist.

Task 2.5

STANDARD INDIRECT COST REPORT

Department: Manufacturing

Period: November 2001

Description	**Favourable variance** £	**Adverse variance** £
Fixed overhead expenditure variance		5,955
Fixed overhead volume variance		6,875
Fixed overhead capacity variance	1,625	
Fixed overhead efficiency variance		8,500

COMMENTS

Fixed overhead expenditure variance £5,955 (A)

The most likely reason for the adverse overhead expenditure variance was an increase in the cost of services used. For example, other property overheads had actual expenditure which was more than twice the budgeted overhead expenditure. Perhaps business rates or buildings insurance costs were significantly higher than budgeted.

Fixed overhead capacity variance £1,625 (F)

This favourable variance may have arisen because extra overtime was worked by the labour force or because more employees were taken on.

Fixed overhead efficiency variance £8,500 (A)

This adverse variance indicates that output was not produced as quickly as expected possibly because of the use of sub-standard materials or poorly trained workers.

Task 2.6

Product: Rosy glow	**Production**	
Production volume	5,000 metres £	6,000 metres £
Depreciation *	1,000	1,000
Rent *	3,200	3,200
Other property overheads *	400	400
Indirect staff costs *	1,400	1,400
White cloth (W1)	11,010	13,212
Red dye (W2)	4,000	4,800
Direct labour (W3)	1,500	1,800
Total cost	22,510	25,812
Cost per 100 metres	450.20	430.20

* Fixed costs – therefore the same cost is incurred for production volumes of both 5,000 and 6,000 metres in January.

Workings

(W1) **White cloth**

$$\text{Cost for 5,000 metres} = \frac{£220.20}{100} \times 5{,}000 \text{ metres} = £11{,}010$$

$$\text{Cost for 6,000 metres} = \frac{£220.20}{100} \times 6{,}000 \text{ metres} = £13{,}212$$

(W2) **Red dye**

$$\text{Cost for 5,000 metres} = \frac{£80}{100} \times 5{,}000 \text{ metres} = £4{,}000$$

$$\text{Cost for 6,000 metres} = \frac{£80}{100} \times 6{,}000 \text{ metres} = £4{,}800$$

(W3) **Direct labour**

$$\text{Cost for 5,000 metres} = \frac{£30}{100} \times 5{,}000 \text{ metres} = £1{,}500$$

$$\text{Cost for 6,000 metres} = \frac{£30}{100} \times 6{,}000 \text{ metres} = £1{,}800$$

Lecturers' resource pack activities

CHAPTER 1: COST INFORMATION

1 PRIME COST — Pre-assessment

Prime cost is

A all costs incurred in manufacturing a product
B the total of direct costs
C the material cost of a product
D the cost of operating a department

2 HOSPITAL — Assessment

(a) Suggest two suitable cost centres for a hospital.
(b) Suggest two suitable cost units for a hospital.

CHAPTER 2: MATERIALS

3 RISING PRICES — Pre-assessment

In a period of rising prices which of the following methods of pricing issues would place the lowest value on the closing stocks?

(a) Weighted average
(b) FIFO
(c) LIFO

4 EXPLAIN — Assessment

Explain how the term 'reorder level' differs from 'minimum level' and 'maximum level'.

5 SYSTEM OF NUMBERS — Assessment

What are the main advantages of using a system of numbers to identify stock held?

CHAPTER 3: LABOUR COSTS

The data below relate to lecturers' practice activities 6-8.

Virgo Ltd is a printing company which pays its employees an individual production bonus of 10p per 100 sheets produced. The normal working week is 38 hours.

6 SINGH AND SMITH — Assessment

Calculate the gross wages earned for each of the following employees for week 32.

	Singh	*Smith*
Basic rate per hour	£4.50	£4.00
Total hours worked	$39\frac{1}{2}$	41
Overtime hours paid:		
at time plus a third	$1\frac{1}{2}$	1
at time plus a half	-	2
Output (sheets)	10,500	10,900

(Calculations should be to two decimal places of a £.)

7 PIECEWORK SYSTEM — Assessment

There has been some pressure from the employees for a piecework system to be introduced.

What would the piecework price per 100 sheets have to be, to at least equal the gross wages earned by Singh in lecturers' practice activity 6 above, assuming the same output level of 10,500 sheets?

(Calculations should be to two decimal places of a £.)

8 OVERTIME PREMIUM — Assessment

The overtime premium paid to Singh and Smith in lecturers' practice activity 6 could be analysed to direct wages or to departmental overheads. Detail the circumstances which would give rise to these differing treatments.

CHAPTER 4: EXPENSES

9 DEPRECIATION Assessment

At the beginning of June 20X9, Libra Ltd purchases a new machine for £17,580. It has not yet been established whether the machine is to be depreciated on a straight line basis over five years or on a 25% reducing balance basis.

Calculate the annual depreciation which would be charged over the next five years under the two methods. Assume a zero residual value for the straight line method.

CHAPTER 5: OVERHEADS AND ABSORPTION COSTING

10 LAST PERIOD **Assessment**

The overheads of a cost centre were substantially over absorbed last period.

(a) What is the costing treatment for this?

(b) Will the costing adjustment increase or decrease the costing profit for the period?

11 SUITABILITY **Assessment**

Suggest suitable cost drivers for the following cost pools.

Production scheduling costs
Despatch costs

12 APPROPRIATE BASIS **Assessment**

Suggest an appropriate basis for apportioning each of the following overhead costs to production cost centres in a manufacturing company.

(a) Canteen costs

(b) Heating and lighting

(c) Building maintenance

CHAPTER 6: COST BEHAVIOUR

13 GOOD BEHAVIOUR **Pre-assessment**

Fill in the gaps for each of the graph titles below.

(a)

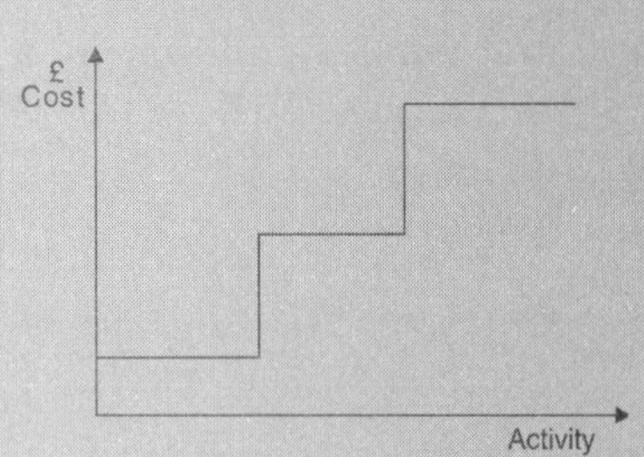

Graph of a .... cost

Example:

(b)

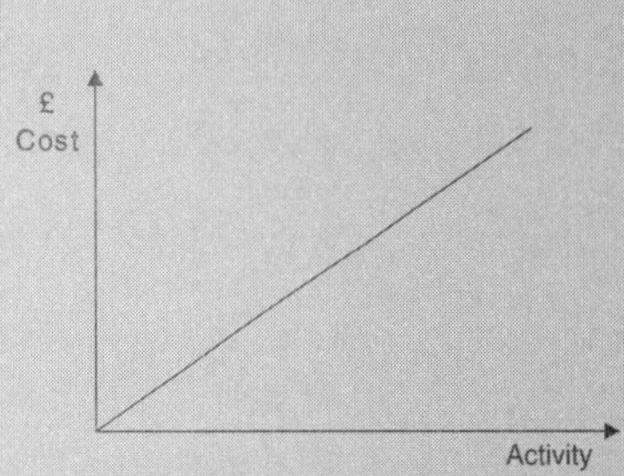

Graph of a .... cost

Example:

(c)

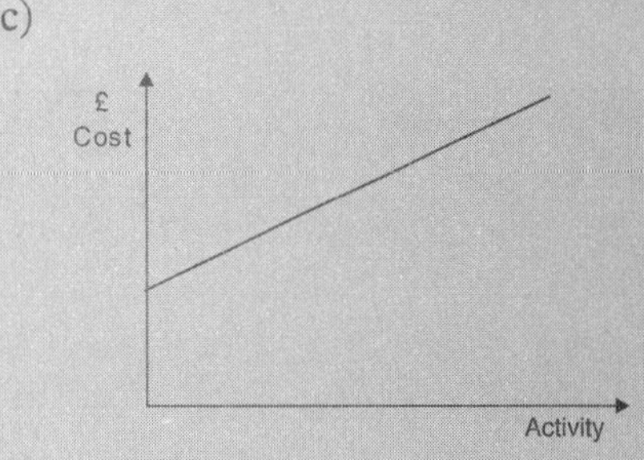

Graph of a .... cost

Example:

(d)

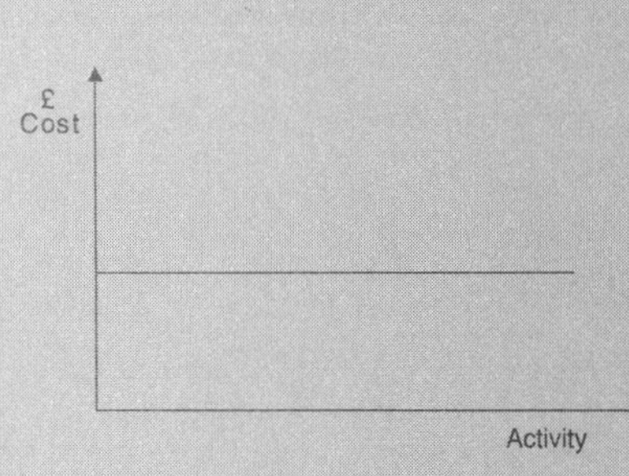

Graph of a .... cost

Example:

14 EAT A LOT **Assessment**

The costs of operating the canteen at the Eat a lot Company for the past three months are as follows.

Month	*Cost*	*Employees*
	£	
1	72,500	1,250
2	75,000	1,300
3	68,750	1,175

Variable cost (per employee per month) =

Fixed cost per month =

CHAPTER 7: BOOKKEEPING ENTRIES FOR COST INFORMATION

The following data relate to lecturers' practice activities 15-19.

(NB. Answer these activities in sequence as the answers to earlier activities may need to be used later.)

Exeter Ltd operates a job costing system which is fully integrated with the financial accounts. The following data relate to May 20X9.

	£
Balances at the beginning of the month	
Stores ledger control account	8,000
Work in progress control account	15,000
Finished goods control account	22,000
Prepayments of production overheads, brought forward from April 20X9	1,000
Transactions during the month	
Materials purchased	75,000
Materials issued to production	34,000
Materials issued to factory maintenance	4,000
Materials transferred between jobs	3,500
Total wages of direct workers	18,000
Recorded non-productive time of direct workers	2,500
Total wages of indirect production workers (total)	11,000
Other production overheads incurred	16,000
Selling and distribution overheads incurred	12,000
Sales	110,000
Cost of finished goods sold	65,000
Cost of finished goods damaged and scrapped in the month	2,000
Value of work in progress at 31 May 20X9	18,000

Production overhead absorption rate is 200% of direct wages.

15 STORES LEDGER — Assessment

Prepare the stores ledger control account.

16 WORK IN PROGRESS — Assessment

Prepare the work in progress control account.

17 OVERHEAD — Assessment

Calculate the under- or over-absorbed overhead in the month.

18 FINISHED GOODS — Assessment

Prepare the finished goods control account.

19 PROFIT — Assessment

Calculate the profit for May.

CHAPTER 8: COSTING METHODS

20 TWIST AND TERN — Assessment

Twist and Tern Ltd is a company that carries out jobbing work. One of the jobs carried out in February was job 1357, to which the following information relates.

Direct material Y:	400 kilos issued from stores at a cost of £5 per kilo.
Direct material Z:	800 kilos issued from stores at a cost of £6 per kilo.
	60 kilos returned.
Department P:	300 hours of labour, of which 100 hours were done in overtime.
Department Q:	200 hours of labour, of which 100 hours were done in overtime.

Overtime work is carried out normally in Department P, where basic pay is £4 per hour plus an overtime premium of £1 per hour. Overtime work was done in Department Q in February because of a request by the customer of another job for his job to be completed quickly. Basic pay in Department Q is £5 per hour and overtime premium is £1.50 per hour.

Department P had to carry out rectification work which took 20 hours in normal time. These 20 hours are additional to the 300 hours above. This rectification work is normal for a job such as job 1357, and since it was expected, it is included in the direct cost of the job.

Overhead is absorbed at the rate of £3 per direct labour hour in both departments.

Tasks

(a) Calculate the direct materials cost of job 1357.
(b) Calculate the direct labour cost of job 1357.
(c) Calculate the full production cost of job 1357.

21 PROCESS PLANT — Assessment

The process plant division of a group of companies has built a food packaging machine to a customer's requirements. A price of £49,000 had been quoted with the intention of achieving a profit of 25% on the selling price. Information relating to the job is as follows.

Customer	Bond Foods Limited
Customer's order no	7206
Job no	1412
Date work started	5 March 20X8
Date job completed in factory	29 April 20X8
Date delivered	2 May 20X8

	March	April
Materials used		
Machining dept (£4 per kg)	725 kgs	175 kgs
Assembly dept (£10 per kg)	190 kgs	140 kgs
Direct wages rate per hour		
Machining dept	£4	£4.40
Assembly dept	£5	£5.25
	Hours	*Hours*
Direct labour hours		
Machining dept	200	100
Assembly dept	50	500
Machine hours in machining dept	350	180
Technical drawings (direct cost)	£2,115	

Production overhead is absorbed at the predetermined rate of £10 per direct labour hour in the assembly department and £15 per machine hour in the machining department.

Commissioning costs, that is installation and initial running-in of the machine at the customer's site, were £750 and these are to be treated as a direct production cost.

Selling and general administration costs are charged to jobs at the rate of $33^1/_3$% of production cost.

Task

Using the information above, complete the job cost card on the following page.

JOB COST CARD		Job No.
Customer	Customer's Order No.	Start Date
Job Description		Delivery Date
Estimate Ref.	Invoice No.	
Quoted price	Invoice price	Despatch Note number

Material						Labour								Overheads			
Date	Req. No.	Qty.	Price £	Cost		Date	Labour Anal. Ref.	Cost Ctre	Hrs.	Rate	Bonus	Cost		Hrs	OAR	Cost	
				£	p							£	p			£	p
Total C/F						Total C/F								Total C/F			

Expenses				
Date	Ref.	Description	Cost	
			£	p
Total C/F				

Job Cost Summary	Actual		Estimate	
	£	p	£	p
Direct Materials B/F Direct Expenses B/F Direct Labour B/F				
Prime Cost Production overheads B/F = Production Cost				
Selling and Admin overhead (33$^1/_3$ of production cost)				
= Total Cost				
Invoice Price				
Job Profit/Loss				

Comments

Job Cost Card Completed by ....

CHAPTER 9: STANDARD COSTING

22 BENDING **Assessment**

The production operation of X plc consists of three departments: bending, cutting and assembly.

(a) Calculate the standard overhead absorption rates for the three departments, selecting the appropriate data.

	Bending	*Cutting*	*Assembly*
Actual overheads	£128,000	£80,000	£64,500
Budgeted overheads	£120,000	£90,000	£60,000
Actual machine hours	11,800	2,750	-
Budgeted machine hours	10,000	3,000	-
Actual labour hours	-	-	15,900
Budgeted labour hours	-	-	15,000

(b) Using the information given below and the standard overhead rates calculated in (a), calculate the standard cost of producing 100 wheels for a toy car.

	Bending	*Cutting*	*Assembly*
Labour rates of pay per hour	£4	£6	£5
Labour hours per 100 wheels	0.8	0.5	1.2
Machine hours per 100 wheels	0.4	0.5	-

STANDARD COST CARD

Toy car wheels Part number 5917B Date:

Standard quantity 100 wheels

	Performance standard	Standard rate/price	Standard cost £
Direct materials			
Tyres	100	10p each	
Steel strip	50	£10.40 per 100	
Wire	1000	2p each	
Direct labour	hours	£	
Bending			
Cutting			
Assembly			
Overheads			
Bending			
Cutting			
Assembly			
TOTAL COST			

23 TARGET SELLING PRICE — Assessment

Using the standard cost card from lecturers' practice activity 22, calculate the target selling price per 100 wheels if the company expects a profit of 10% of the target selling price.

24 100 WHEELS — Assessment

(a) How would the standard labour hours for producing 100 wheels be determined?

(b) The costs of the stores and the personnel department have to be apportioned across the other cost centres. What bases would you recommend?

25 STANDARDS — Assessment

When setting the standard cost of the various products it produces, management must decide whether to use ideal standards or current standards. State which of the two standards you would recommend management to use and explain why.

CHAPTER 10: CALCULATION OF VARIANCES

26 EXPLANATION — Pre-assessment

The organisation you work for, a manufacturing company, revises its standard costs at the beginning of each year. Because of inflation, it sets its standard price for materials at the estimated price level for the middle of the year. During one control period, a fairly large favourable direct material price variance was reported. Which one of the following would *not* help to explain this variance?

A The control period was early in the year.
B Direct materials were purchased in greater bulk than normal.
C An alternative source of supply for materials was found and used.
D Discounts were taken from suppliers for early settlement of invoices.

27 VOLE — Assessment

Testing Ltd manufactures one product, the Vole. The following direct standard costs apply to the Vole.

	£
Direct material 15 kgs at £6 per kg	90
Direct labour 4 hours at £5 per hour	20

In April production was 20,000 units and actual data for the month were:

(a) Actual materials consumed 320,000 kgs costing £1,980,000
(b) Actual labour hours worked 72,000 hours, costing £340,000

Task

Calculate the material price and usage variances, and the labour rate and efficiency variances.

28 AUSTRALIA LTD — Assessment

Australia Ltd produces and sells one product only, the Boomerang, the standard cost for one unit being as follows.

	£
Direct material X - 8 kilograms at £25 per kg	200
Direct material Y - 3 litres at £10 per litre	30
Direct wages - 4 hours at £12.50 per hour	50
Fixed overhead	50
Total standard cost	330

The fixed overhead included in the standard cost is based on an expected monthly output of 2,000 units. Fixed overhead is absorbed on the basis of direct labour hours.

During September 20X8 the actual results were as follows.

Production	1,800 units
Material X	14,800 kg used, costing £390,000
Material Y	6,200 litres used, costing £67,000
Direct wages	8,200 hours worked for £105,000
Fixed overhead	£97,500

Tasks

(a) Calculate price and usage variances for each material.

(b) Calculate labour rate and efficiency variances.

(c) Calculate fixed overhead expenditure and volume variances and then subdivide the volume variance.

29 BARBER LTD — Assessment

Barber Ltd expected to produce 28,000 units of its product the Joely during July 20X8. The standard time for a unit of the product is 4 hours and the budgeted fixed overhead was £140,000. Production overheads are absorbed on the basis of hours worked.

In the event the actual fixed overhead expenditure was £135,000. The number of hours worked was 92,500 and 24,000 units were produced.

Task

Calculate all of the fixed overhead variances for July 20X8.

CHAPTER 11: FURTHER ASPECTS OF VARIANCE ANALYSIS

30 BINDING — Assessment

The binding department of a publishing company had output last period of 1,200 copies of one manual 'AATA'. The standard cost of this manual is shown below.

Standard Cost Card

Product: Manual AATA — **Date prepared:** April 20X9

Element	*Performance Standard*	*Standard Rate/Price*	*Std Cost* £
Direct material	1 unit	90p per unit	0.90
Direct labour	¼ hour	£4 per hour	1.00
Variable overheads	¼ hour	£2 per hour	0.50
Fixed overheads	¼ hour	£6 per hour	1.50
		Cost per manual	£3.90

Complete the following departmental operating account, using the information from the standard cost card above to calculate the standard cost and the total variance for each element of cost. Each variance must be marked 'adverse' (A) or 'favourable' (F).

Departmental Operating Account

Month: May 20X9 — **Budget hours**: 300 — **Department**: Binding
Date prepared: 10.6.X9 — **Actual hours**: 290 — **Manager**: Mrs Jones

Actual Costs	£	*Standard Costs* *Output (Manuals)*	*Unit Cost* £	*Total Cost* £	*Total Variance* £
Direct materials	1,200	1,200			
Direct labour:					
290 hours	1,300	1,200			
Variable overheads	580	1,200			
Fixed overheads	1,920	1,200			
Total	5,000				

31 SUB VARIANCES — Assessment

(a) Analyse the direct labour cost variance in lecturers' practice activity 30 above into the appropriate sub variances.

(b) Suggest one reason for each of the sub variances occurring and outline the corrective action that needs to be taken in each case.

(c) Who would be responsible for taking the corrective action in (b) above?

32 OVERHEAD VARIANCES — Assessment

From lecturers' practice activity 30, name one overhead variance that you would expect to find in the binding department. Explain whether it would be adverse or favourable. (Calculations are not required.)

Lecturers' practice devolved assessment

Lecturers' practice devolved assessment Country Custom Kitchens

Performance criteria

The following performance criteria are covered in this lecturers' practice devolved assessment.

Element 6.1: Record and analyse information relating to direct costs

1. Direct costs are identified in accordance with the organisation's costing procedures
2. Information relating to direct costs is clearly and correctly coded, analysed and recorded
3. Direct costs are calculated in accordance with the organisation's policies and procedures
4. Standard costs are compared against actual costs and any variances are analysed
5. Information is systematically checked against the overall usage and stock control practices
6. Queries are either resolved or referred to the appropriate person

Notes on completing the Assessment

This Assessment is designed to test your ability to record and analyse information relating to direct costs.

You are provided with data on Pages 278 to 292 which you must use to complete the tasks on Page 278-279.

You are allowed **three hours** to complete your work.

A high level of accuracy is required. Check your work carefully.

Correcting fluid should not be used. Errors should be crossed out neatly and clearly. You should write in ink - not pencil.

Do not turn to the suggested answer until you have completed all parts of the Assessment.

A FULL ANSWER TO THIS ASSESSMENT IS PROVIDED IN THE LECTURERS' RESOURCE PACK FOR UNIT 6.

COUNTRY CUSTOM KITCHENS

Data

Following a chip-pan fire in its warehouse showroom, the computerised stock control system of Country Custom Kitchens is out of action. The management of Country Custom Kitchens has called in your firm to help restore the system and you and a number of your colleagues have been delegated the task of keeping the system running manually while the computer system and records are being rebuilt. This is likely to take up to two weeks.

When you arrive on Monday 6 September you find that you are to look after raw materials stocks in the code range A - F (screws and fixings). You are given the A - F part of the daily stock list which was run on the evening before the fire. No transactions have been posted since then. The stock list gives the usual details and also has an 'exceptions' column signalling stocks that need to be reordered. The cost accountant has left you a note about this (she suffered minor burns and is recuperating).

You are handed a pile of documents received or generated that morning. You sort the documents into separate piles and find that you have the following:

(a) The stock list

(b) Several invoices

(c) A number of goods received notes (all of which match their attached purchase orders) for that morning's deliveries

(d) Some materials requisition notes

(e) The note from the cost accountant

Tasks

Using the documents and information on the following pages, complete the tasks outlined below.

(a) Make out stores record cards as necessary and write them up in the light of the documents that you have been given. There is no need to enter control levels on the stores record cards, but otherwise see that all documents (including the materials requisitions) are as complete as possible. If you have any queries note them down on a queries schedule.

(b) (i) Peruse the stock list and make out purchase requisitions for any items that need to be reordered.

(ii) Suggest a way of ensuring that stocks that you requisition are not ordered again once the computer system is restored.

Again, if you are unsure of anything make a note of it.

(c) Peruse the stock list generally and note down on your queries schedule any points that you think need to be brought to the attention of the warehouse manager or the chief purchasing officer.

(d) Prepare journal entries for posting the invoices to the integrated accounts at actual cost. (Do not prepare entries for variances.)

(e) Calculate any variances that have arisen.

(f) Note on your queries schedule any other matters that you think need to be referred to other persons.

(g) Prepare a schedule of materials issued for job costing purposes.

Documents for use in the solution

The documents you will need to prepare a solution are given on Pages 293 to 304 and consist of the following.

(a) Materials requisitions (to be completed)
(b) 12 blank stores record cards
(c) 7 blank purchase requisitions
(d) 1 blank looseleaf journal page
(e) 1 blank query schedule

COUNTRY CUSTOM KITCHENS STOCK LIST 03/09/X3											03/09/X3/ 17:52		
CODE	DESCRIPTION		FACTOR/UNIT	SUPPLIER	COST	IN	OUT	ORDERED	BALANCE	EXCE-PTION	TRANSACTIONS PREV.TOTAL	HISTORY PREV.CUM.	CURRENT CUM.
A0080	SCREW AND NUT	50mm	5	28043112	0.49				58		562	421	383
A0090	SCREW AND NUT	60mm	5	28043112	0.53				63		668	455	445
A1010	WING NUT	M4	5	27561297	0.40				38		452	263	289
A1020	WING NUT	M5	5	27561297	0.40				68		666	454	363
A1030	WING NUT	M6	5	27561297	0.45				54		523	370	362
A1040	WING NUT	M8	5	27561297	0.50				34		360	236	259
A1050	SUPANUT	M4	10	23344248	0.27			10	7		166	124	148
A1060	SUPANUT	M5	10	23344248	0.30		20		48		571	389	353
A1070	SUPANUT	M6	10	23344248	0.32				95		1007	587	469
A1080	SUPANUT	M8	10	23344248	0.37	80			88		862	587	645
A1090	SUPANUT	M10	5	23344248	0.40	70			86		834	549	439
A2010	WASHER	15mm	50	28043112	0.25	70			82		976	732	717
A2020	WASHER	20mm	50	28043112	0.30	70			32		339	197	157
A2030	WASHER	25mm	50	28043112	0.33				70		679	480	528
A2040	WASHER	30mm	20	28043112	0.37				99		1049	715	650
A2050	WASHER	35mm	10	28043112	0.30	80			59		578	380	456
A2060	WASHER BRASS	15mm	10	28043112	0.40				1		740	493	487
A2070	WASHER BRASS	20mm	5	27561247	0.45		60		13		605	393	399
A2080	WASHER BRASS	25mm	5	27561247	0.50		30		62		607	429	343
A2090	WASHER BRASS	30mm	5	27561247	0.55				86	***	1023	596	655
A3010	SELF-TAP BRASS	15mm	10	23344248	0.21	80			16	***	170	127	115
A3020	SELF-TAP BRASS	20mm	10	23344248	0.24			15	17		148	100	98
A3030	SELF-TAP BRASS	25mm	10	23344248	0.27				52		509	335	368
A3040	SELF-TAP	30mm	10	23344248	0.30				74		647	441	529
A3050	SELF-TAP	35mm	10	23344248	0.33			80	18		1166	680	618
A3060	SELF-TAP	40mm	5		0.30				40		350	247	242
A3070		45mm	5		0.33				72		698	523	271
A3080		50mm	5		0.36				61		647	425	510
A3090		60mm	5	23344248	0.39				21		183	124	136
A4010		15mm	10	23344248	0.22				61		591	344	337
A4020	SELF-TAP	20mm	10	23344248	0.24				57		678	480	528
A4030	SELF-TAP	25mm	10	23344248	0.26				74		725	477	434
A4040	SELF-TAP	30mm	10	23344248	0.28		50		13	***	760	500	475

COUNTRY CUSTOM KITCHENS STOCK LIST 03/09/X3													03/09/X3/ 17:52
CODE	DESCRIPTION		FACTOR/UNIT	SUPPLIER	COST	IN	OUT	ORDERED	BALANCE	EXCE-PTION	TRANSACTIONS PREV. TOTAL	HISTORY PREV. CUM.	CURRENT CUM.
A4050	ROUNDHEAD	35mm	10	28043112	0.30				78		827	544	533
A4060	ROUNDHEAD	40mm	5	23344248	0.20			30	10		372	279	223
A4070	ROUNDHEAD	45mm	5	23344248	0.24			75	50		892	520	572
A4080	ROUNDHEAD	50mm	5	23344248	0.28		50		12	***	800	520	533
A4090	ROUNDHEAD	60mm	5	23344248	0.32			40	15		481	316	309
A5010	CROSSHEAD	15mm	10	27561297	0.18				66		785	535	588
A5020	CROSSHEAD	20mm	10	27561297	0.19				80		784	555	505
A5030	CROSSHEAD	25mm	10	27561297	0.20	100			131		1389	914	895
A5040	CROSSHEAD	30mm	10	27561297	0.21				84		823	617	678
A5050	CROSSHEAD	35mm	10	27561297	0.23				76		737	429	343
A5060	CROSSHEAD	40mm	5	28043112	0.17				25		298	211	232
A5070	CROSSHEAD	45mm	5	28043112	0.20				21		205	134	107
A5080	CROSSHEAD	50mm	5	28043112	0.24				96		840	572	632
A5090	CROSSHEAD	60mm	5	28043112	0.30				93		985	544	1182
A6010	BRASS	15mm	10	29295001	0.35				96		940	705	641
A6020	BRASS	20mm	10	29295001	0.39				32		310	204	199
A6030	BRASS	25mm	10	29295001	0.41				36		428	303	333
A6040	BRASS	30mm	10	29295001	0.43				96		941	548	438
A6050	BRASS	35mm	10	29295001	0.46				57		552	376	342
A6060	BRASS	40mm	5	29295001	0.46			40	21		492	340	341
A6070	BRASS	45mm	10	29295001	0.56			5	48		610	400	417
A6080	BRASS	50mm	5	29295001	0.62				77		916	603	482
A6090	BRASS	60mm	5	29295001	0.74				72		705	480	436
*****													
B0010	RLH NAILS	20mm	1kg	23344248	2.69				74		148	148	0
B0020	RLH NAILS	25mm	1kg	23344248	2.69				51		153	153	0
B0030	RLH NAILS	30mm	1kg	23344248	2.69		4	10	0		107	72	79
B0040	RLH NAILS	35mm	1kg	23344248	2.79				24		235	154	150
B0050	RLH NAILS	40mm	1kg	23344248	2.79		6		16		155	109	186
B0060	RLH NAILS	45mm	1kg	23344248	2.99				56		666	388	353
B0070	RLH NAILS	50mm	1kg	23344248	2.99				27		264	173	138
B0080	N/A												
B0090	N/A												

COUNTRY CUSTOM KITCHENS STOCK LIST 03/09/X3												03/09/X3/ 17:52	
CODE	DESCRIPTION		FACTOR/UNIT	SUPPLIER	COST	IN	OUT	ORDERED	BALANCE	EXCEPTION	TRANSACTIONS PREV. TOTAL	HISTORY PREV. CUM.	CURRENT CUM
B1010	RW NAILS	15mm	1kg	27314295	2.60				40		424	280	130
B1020	RW NAILS	20mm	1kg	27314295	2.60				49		568	520	212
B1030	RW NAILS	25mm	1kg	27314295	2.60				19		186	139	136
B1040	RW NAILS	30mm	1kg	27314295	2.60				29		281	184	167
B1050	RW NAILS	35mm	1kg	27314295	2.90				22		262	152	314
B1060	RW NAILS	40mm	1kg	27314295	2.90				12		105	74	81
B1070	RW NAILS	45mm	1kg	27314295	2.99		5	60	11		695	457	447
B1080	RW NAILS	50mm	1kg	27314295	3.05				61		85	179	7
B1090		60mm	1kg		3.15				93		200	266	292
B2010	PANEL PINS	15mm	500g	27561297	1.89				34		405	101	111
B2020	PANEL PINS	20mm	500g	27561297	1.89				14		135	250	268
B2030	PANEL PINS	25mm	500g	27561297	1.99		35		42		403	249	273
B2040	PANEL PINS	30mm	500g	27561297	1.99				49		428	243	238
B2050	PANEL PINS	35mm	500g	27314295	1.99				30		357	69	75
B2060	PANEL PINS	40mm	500g	27314295	2.15		4		11		106	157	125
B2070	PANEL PINS	45mm	500g	27314295	2.15			20	2		222	45	54
B2080	PANEL PINS	50mm	500g	27314295	2.40				7		61	242	266
B2090	PANEL PINS	60mm	500g	27314295	2.40				31		369	118	54
*****													
D0010	BUTT HINGE	40mm	5PR	26134906	1.89	15			89		180	16	1
D0020	BUTT HINGE	50mm	5PR	26134906	2.70				0		16	18	0
D0030	BUTT HINGE	65mm	5PR	26134096	3.45				2	***	195	171	19
D0040	BUTT HINGE	75mm	5PR	26134096	5.27				26	***	252	167	163
D0050	BUTT HINGE	100mm	5PR	26134096	9.99				26		254	92	104
D0060	BUTT CHR	40mm	5PR	23344248	3.14				11		131	146	143
D0070	BUTT CHR	50mm	5PR	23344248	3.73				22		192	265	241
D0080	BUTT CHR	75mm	5PR	23344248	6.84				38		403	118	141
D0090	BUTT CHR	100mm	5PR		11.87				18		174	45	49
D1010	RISING BUTT	40mm	5PR		1.70				8		78	29	0
	RISING BUTT	50mm	5PR	23344248	2.20		10		3		38	43	2
		65mm	5PR	26134906	2.56			10	2	***	47	109	119
D1020		75mm	5PR	26134906	4.32				19		166	75	73
D1030	RISING BUTT	100mm	5PR	26134906	8.87				9		107	68	0
D1040	RISING BUTT			26134906									
D1050	RISING BUTT			26134906									

COUNTRY CUSTOM KITCHENS STOCK LIST 03/09/X3												03/09/X3/ 17:52	
CODE	DESCRIPTION		FACTOR/UNIT	SUPPLIER	COST	IN	OUT	ORDERED	BALANCE	EXCEPTION	TRANSACTIONS PREV. TOTAL	HISTORY PREV. CUM.	CURRENT CUM
D1060	RIS BUTT CHR	40mm	5PR	23344248	2.99				14		148	111	133
D1070	RIS BUTT CHR	50mm	5PR	23344248	3.49				17		164	107	97
D1080	RIS.BUTT CHR	75mm	5PR	23344248	7.50				17		166	113	110
D1090	RIS BUTT CHR	100mm	5PR	23344248	12.00				15		131	76	83
D2010	LIFT OFF BUTT	40mm	5PR	21840027	3.07	10			30		357	267	213
D2020	LIFT OFF BUTT	50mm	5PR	21840027	3.99				38		368	242	237
D2030	LIFT OFF BUTT	65mm	5PR	21840027	4.58				2	***	204	130	140
D2040	LIFT OFF BUTT	75mm	5PR	21840027	6.90		20		19		201	137	124
D2050	LIFT OFF BUTT	100mm	5PR	21840027	12.00				13		127	74	72
D2060	L/O BUTT CHROME	40mm	5PR	23344248	4.05			20	8		214	151	166
D2070	L/O BUTT CHROME	50mm	5PR	23344248	6.07			10	4		122	80	96
D2080	L/O BUTT CHROME	75mm	5PR	23344248	8.17			10	4		137	102	81
D2090	L/O BUTT CHROME	100mm	5PR	23344248	14.92			10	6		64	37	40
D3010	CRANKED LIFT OFF	38mm	1PR	27561297	1.35		3		8		77	54	52
D3020	EASY HANG	50mm	1PR	29295001	1.45				22		262	172	156
D3030	EASY FIX ANTIQUE	50mm	1PR	27314295	0.99		20	35	0		417	274	328
D3040	CONCEALED	26mm	1PR	28043112	2.59	50			64		627	427	341
D3050	CONCEALED	35mm	1PR	28043112	3.35	75			85		901	593	652
D3060	CONCEALED	170*	1PR	28043112	8.95	50			75		656	464	371
D3070	PIANO	350mm	1	25567840	2.12				33		323	188	184
D3080	PIANO	700mm	1	25567840	3.99				26		309	203	184
D3090	PIANO	900mm	1	25567840	4.35		1		13		126	85	102
*****													
F0010	CAVITY FIXINGS	C23	12	27314295	2.89	60			78		827	563	450
F0020	CAVITY FIXINGS	C29	12	26134906	1.24				30		294	193	212
F0030	CAVITY FIXINGS	H54	12	29295001	1.99				51		607	354	346
F0040	CAVITY FIXINGS	F42	12	25567840	1.59	50		50	73		638	451	410
F0050	PLASTIC PLUGS	25mm	100	27561297	1.19				76		737	485	582
F0060	PLASTIC PLUGS	35mm	100	27561297	1.49	75			90		954	715	786
F0070	PLASTIC PLUGS	40mm	100	27561297	1.99				71		695	405	396
F0080	PLASTIC PLUGS	45mm	100	27561297	2.05				32		361	246	196
F0090	PLASTIC PLUGS	50mm	100	27561297	2.47				50		437	287	287
F1010	END BRACKETS	19mm	1PR	27314295	2.29		4		10		97	68	74

COUNTRY CUSTOM KITCHENS STOCK LIST 03/09/X3													03/09/X3/ 17:52
CODE	DESCRIPTION		FACTOR/UNIT	SUPPLIER	COST	IN	OUT	ORDERED	BALANCE	EXCEPTION	TRANSACTIONS PREV. TOTAL	HISTORY PREV. CUM.	CURRENT CUM
F1020	END BRACKETS	25mm	1PR	27314295	2.47				0	***	148	97	17
F1030	END BRACKETS	25mm	1PR	27314295	2.47			10	4		6	3	90
F1040	CENTRE BRACKET	19mm	1	27314295	1.79		1		2		20	11	10
F1050	CENTRE BRACKET	25mm	1	27314295	2.20		2		2		23	17	20
F1060	STEEL TUBE	19mm	2m	28043112	5.59		1		2		19	12	10
F1070	STEEL TUBE	25mm	2m	28043112	7.07				1	***	14	9	9
F1080	BRASS TUBE	19mm	2m	28043112	8.23				5		43	24	26
F1090	BRASS TUBE	25mm	2m	28043112	10.00				8		85	60	58
F2010	DRAWER RUNNERS		1PR	29295001	2.49				122		1452	955	764
F2020	CORNER FITTINGS		4	29295001	3.29				79		774	527	579
F2030	EXTERNAL ANGLE		2m	23344248	1.65				50		485	282	256
F2040	EXTERNAL ANGLE	19mm	2m	23344248	1.99			200	113		2028	1436	1723
F2050	CLIP ON EDGING	25mm	2m	26134906	2.49				350		3710	2782	3060
F2060	FLAT EDGING		2m	26134906	1.35	300			167		1987	1308	1046
F2070	LIPPED EDGING		2m	26134906	1.55				105		1029	728	662
F2080	DOOR TRACK		2m	26134906	11.79				140		1225	714	785
F2090	SINGLE CHANNEL	17mm	2m	26134906	2.29		20		185		1961	1336	1309
F3010		6mm	2m	26134906	1.15				216		2116	1587	1904
F3020	SINGLE CHANNEL	W	2m	27314295	1.50				175		2083	1371	1247
F3030	S/A TRIM		2m	27314295	1.50		25		220		2620	1747	1654
F3040	S/A TRIM	B	2m	27314295	1.50			125	27		1611	939	1032
F3050	S/A TRIM		4	25567840	1.65				67		649	459	550
F3060	DEC. MOULDINGS		4	25567840	2.29				35		417	274	268
F3070	DEC. CORNERS		4	25567840	4.79			10	7		148	111	101
				25567840									
	DEC. CROWNS												
F3080	DEC. BRACKET		4		3.75				0	***	5	5	1
F3090	DEC. TRIM		2m	25567840	3.99				0	***	12	12	2
F4010	BICYCLE HOOKS		1PR	28043112	0.99				55		533	310	341
F1020	UNIV. HOOKS		1PR	28043112	1.49				46		450	306	244
F4030	CUP HOOKS		4	28043112	0.45				89		778	512	614
F4040	CUP HOOKS BRASSED		4	28043112	0.28				70		679	480	528
F4050	HOOK AND EYES		1	28043112	0.41				923		10984	7231	5073
F4060	SCREW HOOK		1	28043112	0.77	800	400		360		4284	3213	2923
F4070	VINE EYES		10	28043112	1.89		50		40		350	204	199

COUNTRY CUSTOM KITCHENS STOCK LIST 03/09/X3											TRANSACTIONS	HISTORY 03/09/X3/ 17:52	
CODE	DESCRIPTION		FACTOR/UNIT	SUPPLIER	COST	IN	OUT	ORDERED	BALANCE	EXCEPTION	PREV. TOTAL	PREV. CUM.	CURRENT CUM
F4080	SCREWEYES	19mm	25	27314295	0.76			60	12		763	520	624
F4090	SCREWEYES	25mm	25	27314295	0.89				12		116	82	90
F5010	MAGN. CATCH	W	1	27561297	3.99				45		441	300	240
F5020	MAGN. CATCH	B	1	27561297	3.99				44		385	253	229
F5030	MAGN. CATCH	S	1	27561297	3.99				43		512	384	376
F5040	SLIDELATCH	W	1	23344248	4.79				40		388	226	271
F5050	SLIDELATCH	B	1	23344248	4.79			40	7		460	325	357
F5060	THUMBLATCH	W	1	23344248	3.99				36		315	214	194
F5070	THUMBLATCH	B	1	23344248	3.99				37		358	208	166
F5080	AUTOLATCH	W	1	23344248	2.69				36		428	281	275
F5090	AUTOLATCH	B	1	23344248	2.69				68		595	446	490
F6010	PEGCASTORS		4	26134906	2.39				32		310	219	250
F6020	PEGCASTORS	¾"	4	26134906	2.56				8		85	57	51
F6030	PEGCASTORS	1"	4	26134906	2.78				7		61	40	32
F6040	PLATECASTORS	1¼"	4	26134906	2.39				9		78	53	51
F6050	PLATECASTORS	¾"	4	26134906	2.56				5		58	33	36
F6060	PLATECASTORS	1"	4	26134906	2.78				5		48	36	43
F6070	BUGGYWHEEL	1¼"	4	25567840	1.45				9		78	51	46
F6080	BUGGYWHEEL	1½"	4	25567840	1.99			4	5		53	37	29
F6090		2"	4	25567840	3.50			4	6		58	39	42
F7010			1	29295001	0.35				10		118	77	92
F7020	DEC. CASTORS		1	29295001	0.50				35		306	208	189
F7030	TOOLCLIP	20mm	1	29295001	0.46				78		764	445	489
F7040	TOOLCLIP	38mm	1	29295001	0.46				89		943	667	653
F7050	HOSECLIP	20mm	1	29295001	0.53				20		194	127	101
F7060	HOSECLIP	38mm	1		0.18	60			41		401	300	273
F7070	HOSECLIP	50mm	1		0.20				60		525	306	336
	G.CLIP	15mm	1	28043112	0.23				68		809	573	687
	G.CLIP	20mm	1	28043112	0.25				48		465	306	278
F7080	G.CLIP	25mm	1	28043112	0.66				25		245	167	133
F7090	G.CLIP	30mm	2	28043112	1.29				19		166	117	128
F8010	DOORSTOP-CONC		1	21840027	0.75				37		392	258	252
F8020	DOORSTOP-FLEX			21840027									
F8030	DOORSTOP-RUB			21840027									

CHIPPIES Veneers

Splinter's Yard, Glue Street
Deighton

Country Custom Kitchens
Brightwell Road
Croydon

INVOICE

Order N./Ref 2073 | Inv. No. 76298 | Date 03.09.X3

Quantity	Description	Unit Price		Total	
		£	p	£	p
1000	Ash veneer 500cm panels	4	70	4,700	00
		Sub-total		4,700	00
		VAT @ 17.5%		822	50
		Invoice total		5,522	50

VAT Reg: 88458485

PERKALLS
FIXINGS

Pink Street, Dartford, Kent

Country Custom
Kitchens
Brightwell Road
Croydon

INVOICE

Order No./Ref 2072 Inv. No. 1187 Date 03.09.X3

Quantity	Description	Unit Price		Total	
		£	p	£	p
50	F42 R/P	1	68	84	00
4	Buggy wheel	2	07	8	28
		Sub-total		92	28
		VAT @ 17.5%		16	15
		Invoice total		108	43

VAT Reg No: 17128987

KEWANBY SUPPLIES
THE EDGE, OFTOWN, WARE

Country Custom
Kitchens
Brightwell Road
Croydon

INVOICE

O/N - 2178 Inv. No. 87/61743 Date 03.09.X3

Quantity	Description	Unit Price £	Unit Price p	Total £	Total p
15	Self-tap 20mm	0	24	3	60
75	Roundhead 45mm	0	24	18	00
40	Roundhead 60mm	0	35	14	00
80	Self-tap 35mm	0	35	28	00
10	Round lost heads 30mm	2	72	27	20
40	Slide latch (black)	4	95	198	00
10	Chromium lift off 50mm	6	20	62	00
		Sub-total		350	80
		VAT @ 17.5%		61	39
		Invoice total		412	19

VAT Reg No: 09347219

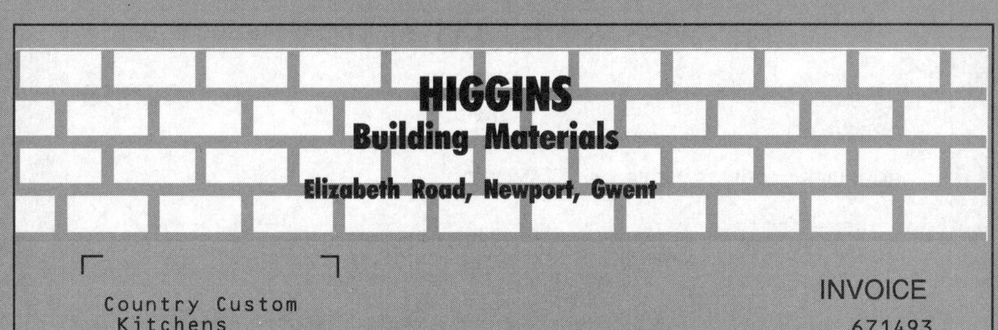

Country Custom Kitchens
Brightwell Road
Croydon
Surrey

INVOICE
671493

Order no. - 2694

Date 03.09.X3

Quantity	Description	Unit Price £	p	Total £	p
20	Panel pins 45mm	2	15	43	00
30	Panel pins 35mm	1	99	59	70
125	Brown self-adhesive trim	1	50	187	50
60	Screw eyes	0	90	54	00
35	Antique hinge 50mm	0	99	34	65
60	Round wire nails 45mm	2	99	179	40
10	End brackets 25mm (pair)	2	47	24	70
		Sub-total		582	95
		VAT @ 17.5%		102	02
		Invoice total		684	97

VAT Reg No: 55252738

GOODS RECEIVED NOTE

WAREHOUSE COPY

DATE: 6.9.X3 TIME: 9.15 NO 24638

ORDER NO: 2164

SUPPLIER'S ADVICE NOTE NO: AN067

QUANTITY	CAT NO	DESCRIPTION
10		Chrome hinges 75mm
		Stock code D2080

RECEIVED IN GOOD CONDITION: JB (INITIALS)

GOODS RECEIVED NOTE

WAREHOUSE COPY

DATE: 6.9.X3 TIME: 9.25 NO 24639

ORDER NO: 2170

SUPPLIER'S ADVICE NOTE NO: PRB/73

QUANTITY	CAT NO	DESCRIPTION
50 (5 packs)		Brass screws 45mm
		Stock code A6070

RECEIVED IN GOOD CONDITION: JB (INITIALS)

GOODS RECEIVED NOTE WAREHOUSE COPY

DATE: 6.9.X3 TIME: 10.10 NO 24670

ORDER NO: 2154

SUPPLIER'S ADVICE NOTE NO: 10423

QUANTITY	CAT NO	DESCRIPTION
10 (4 pkt)	—	Decorative corners
		Stock code: ?

RECEIVED IN GOOD CONDITION: JB (INITIALS)

GOODS RECEIVED NOTE WAREHOUSE COPY

DATE: 6.9.X3 TIME: 11.05 NO 24671

ORDER NO: 2184

SUPPLIER'S ADVICE NOTE NO: NONE

QUANTITY	CAT NO	DESCRIPTION
10 (10 pkt)	—	Super Nut M4
		Stock code: A1050

RECEIVED IN GOOD CONDITION: JB (INITIALS)

GOODS RECEIVED NOTE

WAREHOUSE COPY

DATE: 6.9.X3 TIME: 11.05 NO 24672

ORDER NO: 2184

SUPPLIER'S ADVICE NOTE NO: NONE

QUANTITY	CAT NO	DESCRIPTION
200 (2m lengths)	—	Angle 19mm
		Stock code: F2040

RECEIVED IN GOOD CONDITION: JB (INITIALS)

GOODS RECEIVED NOTE

WAREHOUSE COPY

DATE: 6.9.X3 TIME: 11.05 NO 24673

ORDER NO: 2184

SUPPLIER'S ADVICE NOTE NO: NONE

QUANTITY	CAT NO	DESCRIPTION
30 (5 pkt)	—	Roundhead screws 40mm
		Stock code:

RECEIVED IN GOOD CONDITION: JB (INITIALS)

MATERIALS REQUISITION

Material Required for: *K309/93* No. 0914

(Job or Overhead Account) Date: *6.9.X3*

Quantity	Description	Code No.	Factor/ Unit	Rate	£	Notes
15	*Steel washer 30mm*					

Foreman: *Vlad Kopeii* Costed and Coded:

MATERIALS REQUISITION

Material Required for: *K309/93* No. 0915

(Job or Overhead Account) Date: *6.9.X3*

Quantity	Description	Code No.	Factor/ Unit	Rate	£	Notes
10	*Self-tap 30mm*	*A4040*				

Foreman: *Vlad Kopeii* Costed and Coded:

MATERIALS REQUISITION

Material Required for: *K312/93* No. 0916

(Job or Overhead Account) Date: *6.9.X3*

Quantity	Description	Code No.	Factor/ Unit	Rate	£	Notes
10 chrome	*Butt hinges 40mm*					

Foreman: *VK* Costed and Coded:

MATERIALS REQUISITION

Material Required for: K313/93 (Job or Overhead Account)

No. 0917

Date: 6.9.X3

Quantity	Description	Code No.	Factor/ Unit	Rate	£	Notes
8	Drawer runners					

Foreman: VK

Costed and Coded:

MATERIALS REQUISITION

Material Required for: K313/93 (Job or Overhead Account)

No. 0918

Date: 6.9.X3

Quantity	Description	Code No.	Factor/ Unit	Rate	£	Notes
20	White magnetic catches					

Foreman: Vlad

Costed and Coded:

MATERIALS REQUISITION

Material Required for: K309/93 (Job or Overhead Account)

No. 0919

Date: 6.9.X3

Quantity	Description	Code No.	Factor/ Unit	Rate	£	Notes
2	Panel pins 35mm					

Foreman: VK

Costed and Coded:

STORES RECORD CARD

Material: Maximum Quantity:

Code: Minimum Quantity:

Date	Receipts				Issues				Stock		
	G.R.N. No.	Quantity	Unit Price £	Amount £	Material Req. No.	Quantity	Unit Price £	Amount £	Quantity	Unit Price £	Amount £

STORES RECORD CARD

Material: Maximum Quantity:

Code: Minimum Quantity:

Date	Receipts				Issues				Stock		
	G.R.N. No.	Quantity	Unit Price £	Amount £	Material Req. No.	Quantity	Unit Price £	Amount £	Quantity	Unit Price £	Amount £

STORES RECORD CARD

Material: Maximum Quantity:

Code: Minimum Quantity:

Date	Receipts				Issues				Stock		
	G.R.N. No.	Quantity	Unit Price £	Amount £	Material Req. No.	Quantity	Unit Price £	Amount £	Quantity	Unit Price £	Amount £

STORES RECORD CARD

Material: Maximum Quantity:

Code: Minimum Quantity:

Date	Receipts				Issues				Stock		
	G.R.N. No.	Quantity	Unit Price £	Amount £	Material Req. No.	Quantity	Unit Price £	Amount £	Quantity	Unit Price £	Amount £

STORES RECORD CARD

Material: Maximum Quantity:

Code: Minimum Quantity:

Date	Receipts				Issues				Stock		
	G.R.N. No.	Quantity	Unit Price £	Amount £	Material Req. No.	Quantity	Unit Price £	Amount £	Quantity	Unit Price £	Amount £

STORES RECORD CARD

Material: Maximum Quantity:

Code: Minimum Quantity:

Date	Receipts				Issues				Stock		
	G.R.N. No.	Quantity	Unit Price £	Amount £	Material Req. No.	Quantity	Unit Price £	Amount £	Quantity	Unit Price £	Amount £

STORES RECORD CARD

Material: Maximum Quantity:

Code: Minimum Quantity:

Date	Receipts				Issues				Stock		
	G.R.N. No.	Quantity	Unit Price £	Amount £	Material Req. No.	Quantity	Unit Price £	Amount £	Quantity	Unit Price £	Amount £

STORES RECORD CARD

Material: Maximum Quantity:

Code: Minimum Quantity:

Date	Receipts				Issues				Stock		
	G.R.N. No.	Quantity	Unit Price £	Amount £	Material Req. No.	Quantity	Unit Price £	Amount £	Quantity	Unit Price £	Amount £

STORES RECORD CARD

Material: Maximum Quantity:

Code: Minimum Quantity:

Date	Receipts				Issues				Stock		
	G.R.N. No.	Quantity	Unit Price £	Amount £	Material Req. No.	Quantity	Unit Price £	Amount £	Quantity	Unit Price £	Amount £

STORES RECORD CARD

Material: Maximum Quantity:

Code: Minimum Quantity:

Date	Receipts				Issues				Stock		
	G.R.N. No.	Quantity	Unit Price £	Amount £	Material Req. No.	Quantity	Unit Price £	Amount £	Quantity	Unit Price £	Amount £

STORES RECORD CARD

Material: Maximum Quantity:

Code: Minimum Quantity:

Date	Receipts				Issues				Stock		
	G.R.N. No.	Quantity	Unit Price £	Amount £	Material Req. No.	Quantity	Unit Price £	Amount £	Quantity	Unit Price £	Amount £

STORES RECORD CARD

Material: Maximum Quantity:

Code: Minimum Quantity:

Date	Receipts				Issues				Stock		
	G.R.N. No.	Quantity	Unit Price £	Amount £	Material Req. No.	Quantity	Unit Price £	Amount £	Quantity	Unit Price £	Amount £

PURCHASE REQUISITION Req. No. 10427

Department ______________ Date
Suggested Supplier:

Requested by:

Quantity	Code	Description	Estimated Cost	
			Unit	£

Authorised signature:

PURCHASE REQUISITION Req. No. 10428

Department ______________ Date
Suggested Supplier:

Requested by:

Quantity	Code	Description	Estimated Cost	
			Unit	£

Authorised signature:

PURCHASE REQUISITION Req. No. 10429

Department ______________ Date

Suggested Supplier:

Requested by:

Quantity	Code	Description	Estimated Cost	
			Unit	£

Authorised signature:

PURCHASE REQUISITION Req. No. 10430

Department ______________ Date

Suggested Supplier:

Requested by:

Quantity	Code	Description	Estimated Cost	
			Unit	£

Authorised signature:

PURCHASE REQUISITION Req. No. 10431

Department ________________ Date
Suggested Supplier:

Requested by:

Quantity	Code	Description	Estimated Cost	
			Unit	£

Authorised signature:

PURCHASE REQUISITION Req. No. 10432

Department ________________ Date
Suggested Supplier:

Requested by:

Quantity	Code	Description	Estimated Cost	
			Unit	£

Authorised signature:

PURCHASE REQUISITION Req. No. 10433

Department ________________ Date

Suggested Supplier:

Requested by:

Quantity	Code	Description	Estimated Cost	
			Unit	£

Authorised signature:

Notes from cost accountant on stock list

'Cost' is Standard cost per packet of 10 (or whatever) as shown in the factor column.

In/Out/Balance etc is number of packets (etc) not number of individual items.

Exceptions:
- Stock needing re-ordering
- re-order signalled when less than 1 month's stock on the basis of last year's usage
- re-order qty roughly 1 month's stock (to the nearest five)
- computer over-ridden for slow-moving stock

Prev. total = number of items issued last year

Slow moving stock - we classify stock as slow moving if the current cumulative number of items issued is significantly lower than the previous year's cumulative

NB Friday's deliveries are all posted but system does not update 'ordered' column until next morning (helps with matching invoices)

Otherwise self explanatory

Journal No. _____________

Date	Customer/ supplier code	Invoice	Order No.	Stock code	Quantity	Net £	VAT (17.5%) £

QUERY SCHEDULE

Lecturers' practice central assessment

LECTURERS' PRACTICE CENTRAL ASSESSMENT

This central assessment is in THREE sections. You are reminded that competence must be achieved in each section. You should therefore attempt and aim to complete EVERY task in EACH section.

Essential calculations should be included within your answers where appropriate.

SECTION 1

You are advised to spend approximately 1 hour 15 minutes on this section.

Please note that the tasks should be attempted in numerical order.

The tasks are detailed on pages 307 to 310.

Data

Golden Plum Limited is a small company that bottles and packages specialist jams.

The jam is bought in after the glucose, sugar syrup and fruit extract have been blended and set and passes through the following production departments:

- Inspection
- Bottling
- Packing

The following service departments support these production departments:

- Stores
- Maintenance
- General office

You work as an accounting technician in the general office reporting to the accountant. You have been given a number of tasks concerned with the company's activities for 1999 and 2000.

Task 1.1

There have been several increases recently in the cost of glass jars that are used to bottle jam. The accountant says that she wants these rises reflected in the value of issues from store.

Complete the stores ledger card using the Last-In-First-Out (LIFO) method to cost the issues of glass and value stock for May 1999.

Note. Totals for the value columns for Issues and Balance **must** be shown for each date. Also workings to arrive at values for Issues and Balance should be shown.

STORES LEDGER CARD									
Material:							Month:		
	Receipts			Issues			Balance		
Date	Quantity	Cost (per jar)	Value	Quantity	Cost (per jar)	Value	Quantity	Cost (per jar)	Value
		£	£		£	£		£	£
Balance b/f May 1							48,000	35,600 × 0.12 12,400 × 0.13	5,884
May 6	31,000	0.15	4,650				79,000		
May 9				28,000			51,000		
May 14				37,000			14,000		
May 20	22,500	0.16	3,600				36,500		
May 26				24,000			12,500		

Task 1.2

Golden Plum Limited operates a system of standard costing and variance analysis.

One of your monthly tasks is to assess labour performance in each production department. A cost clerk in the general office has collated the following labour performance statistics for the packing department for May 1999.

Standard time to pack a case	45 seconds
Actual cases packed	102,000
Standard labour hour rate	£6.75 per hour
Actual wages paid	£8,418
Actual hours worked	1,220

Complete the labour variance schedule below to TWO decimal places.

Note the shaded areas should not be filled in but all other boxes should be completed.

LABOUR VARIANCE SCHEDULE			
Department:		Month:	
Variance	*Actual cost*	*Standard cost*	*Variance*
	£	£	£
Labour efficiency			£_______
Labour wage rate			£_______
Total labour cost	£_______	£_______	£_______

Task 1.3

The accountant wants you to complete cost projections for the year ended 31 May 2000 for a special 'Millennium Marmalade' presentation package for which Golden Plum Limited has identified a market.

Investigations have revealed the following.

- Costs are either fixed or variable
- All material costs are variable
- Some labour and overhead costs are fixed and some variable

Complete the table below and calculate the cost per jar for each level of production to TWO decimal places.

BUDGETED PRODUCTION SCHEDULE Product: Year:				
	PRODUCTION (JARS)			
	150,000	175,000	190,000	220,000
COST	£	£	£	£
Material	34,500			50,600
Labour	42,000			47,600
Overhead	60,000			74,000
Total cost	136,500			172,200
Cost per jar (£)				

Task 1.4

The accountant has asked you to do some work on overhead absorption in the production departments for 1999.

From company budgets it has been established that:

- budgeted stores overheads for 1999 are £125,000
- budgeted maintenance overheads for 1999 are £85,600
- the bottling department is to be reapportioned with 45% of the budgeted stores overheads and 40% of the budgeted maintenance overheads
- the packing department is to be reapportioned with 35% of the budgeted stores overheads and 40% of the budgeted maintenance overheads
- the bottling department absorbs overheads on the basis of machine hours
- the packing department absorbs overheads on the basis of labour hours

(a) **Complete the table below to arrive at the budgeted production overhead absorption rates of the bottling and packing departments to TWO decimal places.**

BUDGETED PRODUCTION OVERHEAD SCHEDULE (EXTRACT) YEAR: 1999		
	Bottling department	Packing department
Allocated overheads (£)	85,000	96,000
Apportioned overheads (£)	246,000	194,000
Reapportioned stores overheads (£)		
Reapportioned maintenance overheads (£)		
Total production overheads (£)		
Budgeted machine hours	17,381	11,807
Budgeted labour hours	14,605	16,919
Budgeted production overhead absorption rate (£)		

The accountant wants you to review the absorption of production overheads in the bottling department, for the three months ended May 1999.

The standard time to bottle one jar is 30 seconds and overheads are absorbed on the basis of standard hours produced.

(b) **Complete the schedule below for the bottling department.**

Note: production overheads absorbed should be rounded to the nearest £.

BOTTLNG DEPARTMENT OVERHEAD ABSORPTION SCHEDULE			
	March 1999	April 1999	May 1999
Actual production overheads (£)	31,650	32,398	32,880
Jars bottled	157,392	159,804	163,500
Standard machine hours produced (to one decimal place)			
Budgeted production overhead absorption rate (£)			
Overheads absorbed (£)			
Over/(under) absorbed production overheads (£)			

SECTION 2

You are advised to spend approximately 45 minutes on this section. The tasks are detailed on pages 311 and 314.

Task 2.1

In task 1.1. you calculated the value of the closing stock on May 26 using the Last-In-First-Out method.

(a) **Would the value of the closing stock be higher or lower if the First-In-First-Out (FIFO) method of valuation was used?**

....

(b) **Explain the reason for the difference in the closing stock value between using the First-In-First-Out method and the Last-In-First-Out method of valuation.**

....

....

....

....

....

....

Task 2.2

The accountant is worried because the number of glass jars has gone below the reorder level and a new order has not been placed.

Explain how the reorder level is arrived at.

....

....

....

....

Task 2.3

The materials that come into store are coded for costing purposes.

List two benefits to the company from coding materials

(i) ....

....

(ii) ....

....

Task 2.4

In task 1.2 you calculated the labour sub-variances. Explain how the standard for the labour wage rate might have been arrived at.

....

....

....

....

Task 2.5

Explain what a standard labour hour produced is.

....

....

....

....

....

Task 2.6

The company wishes to calculate labour turnover in the packing department.

(a) **Give a ratio that would express labour turnover.**

....

....

(b) **Give one source of information for labour turnover.**

....

Task 2.7

In task 1.3 costs were classified as being either fixed or variable. Another classification of cost is stepped-fixed.

Sketch in the graph below to show how stepped-fixed costs behave with changes in the level of production and give an example of a stepped-fixed cost.

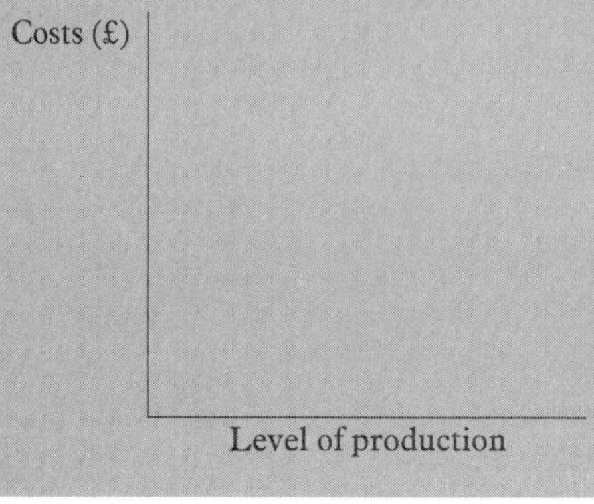

Costs (£)

Level of production

Example of a stepped-fixed cost:

....

Task 2.8

In task 1.3 labour and overhead costs were identified as being either fixed or variable. Give one example of a fixed cost for:

Labour..

Overheads...

Task 2.9

Identify the trend in the cost per jar as production moves from 150,000 to 220,000 jars from your answer to task 1.3 and explain the reason for this trend.

Trend:..

....

....

Explanation for trend: ....

....

....

....

....

....

Task 2.10

In task 1.4 the service cost centres were reapportioned to the production cost centres. Explain why this is done.

....

....

....

....

....

Task 2.11

Below are four types of costs that have been included in task 1.4(a) in either allocated overheads or apportioned overheads for the bottling department.

Identify whether they are an apportioned cost or an allocated cost for the bottling department by circling the appropriate classification.

(i)	**Rent of factory**	Apportioned cost	Allocated cost
(ii)	**Wages of bottling department supervisor**	Apportioned cost	Allocated cost
(iii)	**Maintenance costs of machinery in bottling department**	Apportioned cost	Allocated cost
(iv)	**Insurance of factory buildings**	Apportioned cost	Allocated cost

Task 2.12

Complete the production overhead control account for the bottling department for April 1999 using your answer from task 1.4(b).

PRODUCTION OVERHEAD CONTROL A/C

	£		£

SECTION 3

You are advised to spend approximately 1 hour on this section. The task is detailed on pages 315 and 316.

DATA

The accountant has asked you to review the performance of the bottling department against the budget for January to May 1999.

A cost clerk has calculated the material and labour variances and these have been inserted in the standard cost report on page 316.

The fixed overhead variances have not been calculated. In order to calculate the variances you have collected the following information for the year-to-date in the bottling department.

Budgeted production overheads	£178,359
Budgeted machine hours	7,355
Actual machine hours	6,925
Standard machine hours produced (to nearest hour)	6,659
Actual production overheads	£164,379

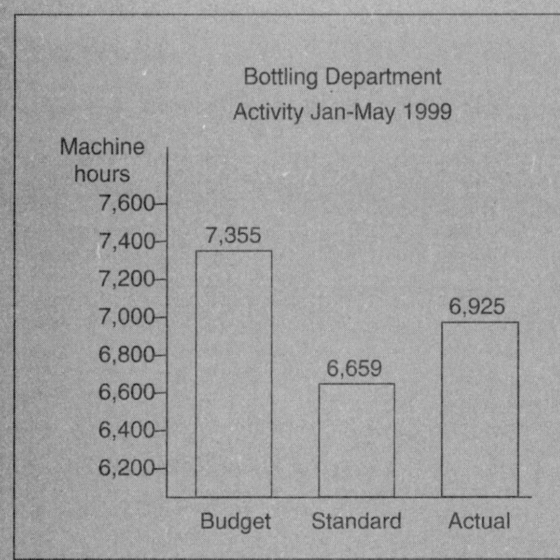

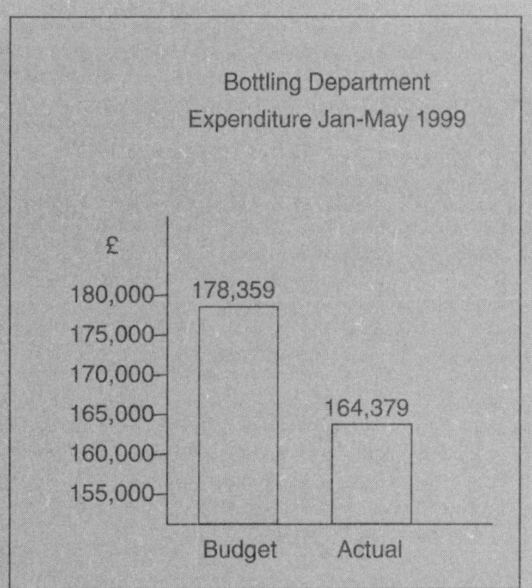

The budgeted production overhead absorption rate should be to TWO decimal places and be calculated on the basis of budgeted machine hours.

The company has been under pressure recently to reduce costs. A proposed pay increase has not been implemented and training of new operatives in the production departments has been reduced. The price of the glass that is provided by the company's only supplier has increased unexpectedly.

Task 3.1

Complete the standard cost report on page 316 by:

- calculating the overhead variances
- summarising the total variances
- listing any sub-variance in excess of £2,500
- commenting on the possible causes of all the material and labour variances and sub-variances from **the information given**
- explaining what the variances for fixed overheads mean and noting any overhead variance that should be brought to the attention of the accountant.

Note. The stationery available on pages 316 and 317 is indicative of the length of report required. However, if you require additional stationery a continuation sheet is available on page 318.

Task 3.1

Notes. Entries should be to the nearest £. Do not complete the shaded boxes.

STANDARD COST REPORT

To: Period:

Description	Sub-variance	Total variance
	£	£
MATERIAL		
Material price	2,840 (A)	
Material usage	390 (A)	
Total material cost		3,230 (A)
LABOUR		
Labour wage rate	890 (F)	
Labour efficiency	2,875 (A)	
Total labour cost		1,985 (A)
OVERHEADS		
Overhead expenditure		
Overhead capacity		
Overhead efficiency		
Overhead volume		
Total overhead cost		

COMMENTS

Task 3.1 (continued)

COMMENTS

CONTINUATION SHEET (This sheet is provided for the continuation of the report. It will not need to be used by all candidates.)

COMMENTS

See overleaf for information on other
BPP products and how to order

AAT Order

To BPP Publishing Ltd, Aldine Place, London W12 8AW
Tel: 020 8740 2211. Fax: 020 8740 1184
E-mail: Publishing@bpp.com Web:www.bpp.com

Mr/Mrs/Ms (Full name)
Daytime delivery address
Postcode
Daytime Tel E-mail

FOUNDATION (£14.95 except as indicated)	**5/02 Texts**	**5/02 Kits**	**Special offer**	**8/02 Passcards**	**Tapes**
Units 1 & 2 Receipts and Payments	☐	☐			
Unit 3 Ledger Balances and Initial Trial Balance	☐			Foundation £6.95 ☐	£10.00 ☐
Unit 4 Supplying Information for Mgmt Control	☐				
Unit 20 Working with Information Technology (£9.95) (6/02)	☐				
Unit 22/23 Healthy Workplace/Personal Effectiveness (£9.95)	☐				
INTERMEDIATE (£9.95)					
Unit 5 Financial Records and Accounts	☐	☐	All	£5.95 ☐	£10.00 ☐
Unit 6 Cost Information	☐	☐	Inter'te Texts	£5.95 ☐	£10.00 ☐
Unit 7 Reports and Returns	☐	☐	and Kits (£65)	£5.95 ☐	
Unit 21 Using Information Technology	☐	☐	☐	£5.95 ☐	
TECHNICIAN (£9.95)					
Unit 8/9 Core Managing Costs and Allocating Resources	☐	☐	Set of 12	£5.95 ☐	£10.00 ☐
Unit 10 Core Managing Accounting Systems	☐	☐	Technician		
Unit 11 Option Financial Statements (A/c Practice)	☐	☐	Texts/Kits	£5.95 ☐	£10.00 ☐
Unit 12 Option Financial Statements (Central Govnmt)	☐	☐	(Please		
Unit 15 Option Cash Management and Credit Control	☐	☐	specify titles	£5.95 ☐	
Unit 16 Option Evaluating Activities	☐	☐	required)	£5.95 ☐	
Unit 17 Option Implementing Auditing Procedures	☐	☐	(£100)	£5.95 ☐	
Unit 18 Option Business Tax (FA02)(8/02 Text & Kit)	☐	☐	☐	£5.95 ☐	
Unit 19 Option Personal Tax (FA 02)(8/02 Text & Kit)	☐	☐		£5.95 ☐	
TECHNICIAN 2001 (£9.95)					
Unit 18 Option Business Tax FA01 (8/01 Text & Kit)	☐	☐			
Unit 19 Option Personal Tax FA01 (8/01 Text & Kit)	☐	☐			
SUBTOTAL	£	£	£	£	£

TOTAL FOR PRODUCTS £

POSTAGE & PACKING

	First	**Each extra**	
Texts/Kits			
UK	£2.00	£2.00	£
Europe*	£4.00	£2.00	£
Rest of world	£20.00	£10.00	£
Passcards			
UK	£2.00	£1.00	£
Europe*	£2.50	£1.00	£
Rest of world	£15.00	£8.00	£
Tapes			
UK	£1.00	£1.00	£
Europe*	£1.00	£1.00	£
Rest of world	£4.00	£4.00	£

TOTAL FOR POSTAGE & PACKING £
(Max £10 Texts/Kits/Passcards)

Grand Total (Cheques to *BPP Publishing*) I enclose a cheque for (incl. Postage) £
Or charge to Access/Visa/Switch
Card Number

Expiry date Start Date

Issue Number (Switch Only)

Signature

We aim to deliver to all UK addresses inside 5 working days; a signature will be required. Orders to all EU addresses should be delivered within 6 working days. All other orders to overseas addresses should be delivered within 8 working days. * Europe includes the Republic of Ireland and the Channel Islands.

REVIEW FORM & FREE PRIZE DRAW

All original review forms from the entire BPP range, completed with genuine comments, will be entered into one of two draws on 31 January 2003 and 31 July 2003. The names on the first four forms picked out on each occasion will be sent a cheque for £50.

Name: ______________________ **Address:** ______________________

____

____

How have you used this Assessment Kit? *(Tick one box only)*

- ☐ Home study (book only)
- ☐ On a course: college ______________
- ☐ With 'correspondence' package
- ☐ Other ______________

Why did you decide to purchase this Assessment Kit? *(Tick one box only)*

- ☐ Have used BPP Texts in the past
- ☐ Recommendation by friend/colleague
- ☐ Recommendation by a lecturer at college
- ☐ Saw advertising
- ☐ Other ______________

During the past six months do you recall seeing/receiving any of the following? *(Tick as many boxes as are relevant)*

- ☐ Our advertisement in *Accounting Technician* magazine
- ☐ Our advertisement in *Pass*
- ☐ Our brochure with a letter through the post

Which (if any) aspects of our advertising do you find useful? *(Tick as many boxes as are relevant)*

- ☐ Prices and publication dates of new editions
- ☐ Information on Interactive Text content
- ☐ Facility to order books off-the-page
- ☐ None of the above

Have you used the companion Interactive Text for this subject? ☐ **Yes** ☐ **No**

Your ratings, comments and suggestions would be appreciated on the following areas

	Very useful	*Useful*	*Not useful*
Introductory section (How to use this Assessment Kit etc)	☐	☐	☐
Practice activities	☐	☐	☐
Practice devolved assessments	☐	☐	☐
Trial run devolved assessments	☐	☐	☐
AAT Sample Simulation	☐	☐	☐
Trial run central assessments	☐	☐	☐
Lecturers' Resource Pack activities	☐	☐	☐
Content of answers	☐	☐	☐
Layout of pages	☐	☐	☐
Structure of book and ease of use	☐	☐	☐

	Excellent	*Good*	*Adequate*	*Poor*
Overall opinion of this Kit	☐	☐	☐	☐

Do you intend to continue using BPP Assessment Kits/Interactive Texts? ☐ Yes ☐ No

Please note any further comments and suggestions/errors on the reverse of this page.

The BPP author of this edition can be e-mailed at: lynnwatkins@bpp.com

Please return to: Nick Weller, BPP Publishing Ltd, FREEPOST, London, W12 8BR

REVIEW FORM & FREE PRIZE DRAW (continued)

Please note any further comments and suggestions/errors below

FREE PRIZE DRAW RULES

1 Closing date for 31 January 2003 draw is 31 December 2002. Closing date for 31 July 2003 draw is 30 June 2003.

2 Restricted to entries with UK and Eire addresses only. BPP employees, their families and business associates are excluded.

3 No purchase necessary. Entry forms are available upon request from BPP Publishing. No more than one entry per title, per person. Draw restricted to persons aged 16 and over.

4 Winners will be notified by post and receive their cheques not later than 6 weeks after the relevant draw date.

5 The decision of the promoter in all matters is final and binding. No correspondence will be entered into.